The Stock Market
Crash of 1929

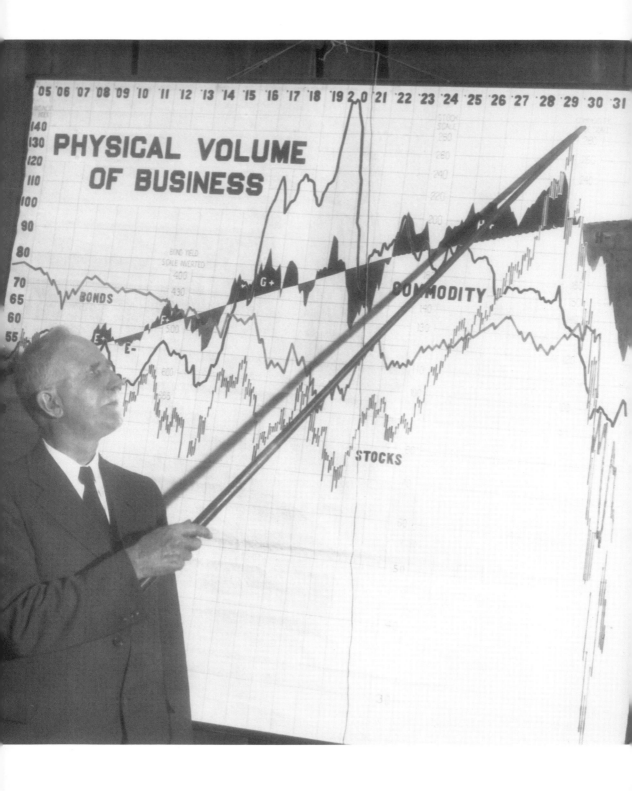

The Stock Market Crash of 1929

Kristine Brennan

CHELSEA HOUSE PUBLISHERS
Philadelphia

Frontispiece: An economist shows how the stock market rose through the 1920s, then "crashed" in 1929, dropping steeply over the next four years.

Cover photos: Corbis/Bettmann-UPI

CHELSEA HOUSE PUBLISHERS

Editor in Chief Stephen Reginald
Production Manager Pamela Loos
Art Director Sara Davis
Director of Photography Judy L. Hasday
Managing Editor James D. Gallagher

Staff for THE STOCK MARKET CRASH OF 1929

Associate Art Director/Designer Takeshi Takahashi
Picture Researcher Patricia Burns
Cover Designer Takeshi Takahashi

First Printing

1 3 5 7 9 8 6 4 2

The Chelsea House World Wide Web address is
http://www.chelseahouse.com

Library of Congress Cataloging-in-Publication Data

Brennan, Kristine, 1969–
The Stock Market Crash / Kristine Brennan
p. cm. — (Great disasters and their reforms)
Includes bibliographical references and index.
Summary: Chronicles the stock market crash of 1929, what led to it, the Great Depression that followed, and measures that were taken to prevent another such crash.

ISBN 0-7910-5268-0

1. Stock Market Crash, 1929 Juvenile literature. 2. Depressions—1929—United States Juvenile literature. 3. United States—Economic conditions—1918–1945 Juvenile literature. 4. United States—Economic policy—1933–1945 States Juvenile literature. [1. Stock Market Crash, 1929. 2. Depressions—1929. 3. United States—Economic conditions—1933–1945.]
I. Title. II. Series.
HB3717 1929.B68 2000
338.5'4'097309043—dc21   99–41974
                                              CIP

Contents

GREAT DISASTERS
REFORMS and RAMIFICATIONS

Jill McCaffrey
National Chairman,
Armed Forces Emergency Services
American Red Cross

Introduction

D isasters have always been a source of fascination and awe. Tales of a great flood that nearly wipes out all life are among humanity's oldest recorded stories, dating at least from the second millennium B.C., and they appear in cultures from the Middle East to the Arctic Circle to the southernmost tip of South America and the islands of Polynesia. Typically gods are at the center of these ancient disaster tales—which is perhaps not too surprising, given the fact that the tales originated during a time when human beings were at the mercy of natural forces they did not understand.

To a great extent, we still are at the mercy of nature, as anyone who reads the newspapers or watches nightly news broadcasts can attest. Hurricanes, earthquakes, tornados, wildfires, and floods continue to exact a heavy toll in suffering and death, despite our considerable knowledge of the workings of the physical world. If science has offered only limited protection from the consequences of natural disasters, it has in no way diminished our fascination with them. Perhaps that's because the scale and power of natural disasters force us as individuals to confront our relatively insignificant place in the physical world and remind us of the fragility and transience of our lives. Perhaps it's because we can imagine ourselves in the midst of dire circumstances and wonder how we would respond. Perhaps it's because disasters seem to bring out the best and worst instincts of humanity: altruism and selfishness, courage and cowardice, generosity and greed.

As one of the national chairmen of the American Red Cross, a humanitarian organization that provides relief for victims of disasters, I have had the privilege of seeing some of humanity's best instincts. I have witnessed communities pulling together in the face of trauma; I have seen thousands of people answer the call to help total strangers in their time of need.

Of course, helping victims after a tragedy is not the only way, or even the best way, to deal with disaster. In many cases planning and preparation can minimize damage and loss of life—or even avoid a disaster entirely. For, as history repeatedly shows, many disasters are caused not by nature but by human folly, shortsightedness, and unethical conduct. For example, when a land developer wanted to create a lake for his exclusive resort club in Pennsylvania's Allegheny Mountains in 1880, he ignored expert warnings and cut corners in reconstructing an earthen dam. On May 31, 1889, the dam gave way, unleashing 20 million tons of water on the towns below. The Johnstown Flood, the deadliest in American history, claimed more than 2,200 lives. Greed and negligence would figure prominently in the Triangle Shirtwaist Company fire in 1911. Deplorable conditions in the garment sweatshop, along with a failure to give any thought to the safety of workers, led to the tragic deaths of 146 persons. Technology outstripped wisdom only a year later, when the designers of the luxury liner *Titanic* smugly declared their state-of-the-art ship "unsinkable," seeing no need to provide lifeboat capacity for everyone onboard. On the night of April 14, 1912, more than 1,500 passengers and crew paid for this hubris with their lives after the ship collided with an iceberg and sank. But human catastrophes aren't always the unforeseen consequences of carelessness or folly. In the 1940s the leaders of Nazi Germany purposefully and systematically set out to exterminate all Jews, along with Gypsies, homosexuals, the mentally ill, and other so-called undesirables. More recently terrorists have targeted random members of society, blowing up airplanes and buildings in an effort to advance their political agendas.

The books in the GREAT DISASTERS: REFORMS AND RAMIFICA-TIONS series examine these and other famous disasters, natural and human made. They explain the causes of the disasters, describe in detail how events unfolded, and paint vivid portraits of the people caught up in dangerous circumstances. But these books are more than just accounts of what happened to whom and why. For they place the disasters in historical perspective, showing how people's attitudes and actions changed and detailing the steps society took in the wake of each calamity. And in the end, the most important lesson we can learn from any disaster—as well as the most fitting tribute to those who suffered and died—is how to avoid a repeat in the future.

Large crowds gathered on Wall Street on October 24, 1929, as word spread that stock prices were falling. Many investors were ruined on "Black Thursday," as that day came to be called; countless others would lose all they had in the weeks to come.

The Bottom Falls Out

—*"Outside the Exchange in Broad Street a weird roar could be heard."*
—John Kenneth Galbraith in *The Great Crash*

On the morning of Thursday, October 24, 1929, a crowd gathered outside the New York Stock Exchange (NYSE). This in itself wasn't unusual. In recent months, investors anxious to put their own fingers on the pulse of the seemingly limitless bull market (a market with rising stock prices) had been arriving as early as 7:00 A.M. to insure themselves a seat in the Stock Exchange's 10,000-seat visitors' gallery. Trading didn't start until 10:00 A.M., but housewives, grocers, seamstresses, and white-collar professionals alike considered it

The New York World, founded by famous newspaper publisher Joseph Pulitzer, trumpeted the frantic news of Wall Street's financial panic, as well as the attempt by a consortium of New York bankers to infuse the market with cash to prop up stock prices.

worth the wait for a chance to play the market.

Most of 1929 had been characterized by a previously undreamed-of surge in stock prices. At parties, in offices, and practically anywhere else people congregated, the conversation turned to the bright prospects of stocks like General Motors, U.S. Steel, and "Radio" (Radio Corporation of America, or RCA). Having ridden the wave of material prosperity that had arrived in the 1920s after World War I, many of those who now found themselves part of the mob outside the NYSE had purchased their stocks on margin, or credit. Their goal was to sell off the shares with a profit left over after paying for the loan they had used to purchase the stock in the first place.

This hope was not entirely unfounded. Despite some shakiness in stock prices throughout the early autumn of 1929, acknowledged financial experts continued to feed the average investor's yearning for easy money. For example, on October 15 Yale economist Irving Fisher had declared, "Stock prices have reached what looks like a permanently high plateau." There were dissenting voices, but listening to them would have meant foregoing the dream of striking it rich. Back in March, another well-known economist named Paul Warburg had urged the Federal Reserve Board to halt stock market speculation in order to prevent a depression that would devastate the nation. Warburg's remarks had provoked reactions ranging from indifference to outright hostility. Bankers and brokers did not want to restrain the great bull market in any way. And few people wanted to believe economist Roger Babson when, at the National Business Conference in Boston on September 5, he predicted, "Sooner or later a crash is coming."

But as investors milled about Wall and Broad Streets on the morning of October 24, a day that would come to be known as "Black Thursday," it is worth wondering whether echoes of Babson's prophetic warning rang in their ears. The people lined up outside the NYSE that day were not waiting just to stroll in and enjoy the usual bustle of buying and selling. For some of them, the next few hours on the floor of the Exchange would make the difference between financial survival and utter ruin.

"On September 3, by common consent, the great bull market of the nineteen-twenties came to an end," wrote John Kenneth Galbraith in *The Great Crash of*

1929. Stock prices were still high—although slowly slipping downhill—throughout the rest of the month. Only a few investors had been farsighted enough in September to sense that the boom was over and that it was time to sell. Many more believed that the slump was only temporary. In fact, as stock price indexes dropped some 50 points (dollars) during the period from early September to mid-October, some people actually bought more stocks. They mistakenly believed that increasing their stock holdings at reduced prices was a shrewd measure that would pay off when the market started charging upward again.

Signs of trouble were there for those who were willing to see them, however. In August of 1929 the Federal Reserve Board, anxious about the number of smaller banks borrowing its funds to finance margin accounts to speculators, had raised the rediscount rate (the fee it charged on its loans to member banks) from 5 to 6 percent. This move seemed to do little more than anger people who resented what they perceived as the government's attempt to throttle the bull market. By October, the New York Stock Exchange was regularly experiencing drops in stock prices, followed by quick recoveries. To both unsophisticated and seasoned investors, these fluctuations seemed to be just "technical corrections." Popular wisdom held that big investors and companies could not afford to let stock prices fall too low. There existed a tacit expectation that these heavy hitters would pool their money and buy large amounts of stock in order to prop up stock prices whenever the market slipped.

In the days preceding Black Thursday, rumors of such "organized support" had been swirling around the Exchange. Small investors anxiously awaited confirmation of these rumors as they filed into the visitor's gallery. But after 10:00 A.M. on October 24, prices continued their downward spiral after a fleeting rally that lasted less than half an hour. Large investors in particular had issued "stop-loss" orders (also called "stop orders") to their brokers. A stop order is an order to automatically sell a particular stock when it reaches a certain level. If the stock is rising, the speculator will get out of the market with a profit. If it is falling, the stop order will keep the investor from holding on to the stock and losing a lot of money.

However, the falling market triggered a large number of stop-loss orders. The sale of huge blocks of stock at low prices touched off a chain reaction of panic. As small investors watched the prices of their stocks plummet after these massive sales, they rushed to bail out of a rapidly sinking market.

The mayhem grew with each passing minute. The trading posts that dotted the NYSE floor's 36,000 square feet were crammed with hollering brokers trying to get their clients' sell orders processed. As brokers collected more and more slips of paper instructing them to sell, some used wastebaskets to hold them all. Attempts to get the latest price quotes were futile: the ticker-tape machines that kept a running record of stock prices based on the latest transactions were simply unable to keep up with the avalanche of sales taking place.

By the time Black Thursday drew to its stunning close at 3:00 P.M., the ticker tape readings would fall approximately four hours behind the actual transactions on the Exchange floor. The ticker-tape machines'

This anxious crowd outside a Wall Street brokerage house was desperate for news about spiraling stock prices—and hopeful that bankers would step in to support the market

sluggishness in the face of rabid selling promised grim ramifications beyond the NYSE. People who were huddled around the ticker-tape machines in brokerage offices around the country became even more confounded than their dazed New York counterparts. As soon as they learned of the frenzy of selling that had begun on Wall Street that morning, they swamped their local brokers with sell orders. These had to be called into the Exchange for processing. By the time out-of-town investors actually sold their stocks, the low prices they had settled for had plunged even lower because of the delay. Time-zone differences only compounded the problem.

Anything seemed possible in this climate of frenzied financial panic. As tensions mounted outside the Exchange that morning, the mob had spied a worker making repairs to a nearby rooftop. Many immediately assumed that the workman was a distraught speculator ready to end his misery. Some people in the crowd—perhaps made more mean-spirited than usual by the looming prospect of their own ruin—urged the man to go ahead and jump; others entreated him to reconsider.

The man remained oblivious to the scene below and finished his work without incident. But at street level, there had been no break in the uneasy climate. Some 500 police and detectives, both mounted and on foot, kept a wary eye on the tense knots of humanity that filled Wall and Broad Streets. In the midst of all these worried investors, however, hope survived into the afternoon. Many still believed that Wall Street's big investment companies would pool their resources to calm the tumbling stock market.

They were right—for the moment. "In New York at least the panic was over by noon. At noon the organized support appeared," noted Galbraith. Even as the crowd waited and hoped, its wish was being granted. The presidents of New York City's four biggest banks—National City Bank, Chase National Bank, Guaranty Trust Company, and Bankers Trust Company—were gathered at the headquarters of J. P. Morgan and Company at 23 Wall Street. This was just a short walk from the Exchange trading floor, which was at 18 Broad Street. As this noontime meeting took place, the ticker was already quoting prices more than 90 minutes behind what they actually were, and rattled investors were selling blindly in order to avoid ending up in worse financial shape than they already were. In short order, the four bank presidents agreed to pump $250 million of their combined funds into the market to encourage other investors to hold on to—or even to buy more of—their stocks, thereby putting the brakes on plummeting prices. After the meeting was adjourned, the bankers set to work immediately, buying large blocks of stock at higher prices than the latest bids. The big investors hoped that their infusion of money would drive up stock prices quickly and permanently.

The bankers' support *did* work quickly. Prices stopped their nosedive as soon as news of the bankers' meeting leaked out. It worked like a magical stabilizing tonic on the floor of the Exchange. By the time the final bell rang at 3:00 P.M., some stocks had actually gained ground.

But for many investors—especially those far from New York—the $250 million rescue of the Stock Exchange came too late. Acting on whatever information they could get, some sold at rock-bottom prices, unaware of the last-minute salvation of the Exchange until long after the floor had closed for the day. In the case of investors who had purchased stock on margin from brokers, it was the brokers who panicked when prices dipped too low to cover their client's debts. Many of those who bought stocks on credit had already had their shares sold out from under them by brokers anxious to cover the credit debt. By the end of the day, the market had firmed up to the point that many of them actually could have kept their stocks. With no way to foresee the late-afternoon stabilization of the market, however, stockholders and their brokers made many regrettable errors.

It was after 7 P.M. before the ticker finished recording the day's transactions. Piles of still-unexecuted orders would ultimately undo some of the bankers' organized support. Brokers and clerks alike toiled through the night to execute all of the sell orders that had piled up that day. In the end, approximately 13 million shares were bought and sold—with the emphasis on selling. (To put this staggering number into perspective, during the peak of the 1929 bull market, a brisk day was one during which 4 million shares changed hands.)

On Wall Street, the lights burned brightly into the morning of Friday, October 25. Most brokers got little or no sleep as they tried to make sense of what had happened during the previous day's trading. The only people who seemed unaffected were errand boys and messengers who had had nothing invested in the market. They poured excitedly into the New York City streets, energized by the chaos that had surrounded them. Hotels rolled out temporary sleeping quarters for overwhelmed brokers and clerks so that they could work into the wee hours, grab a catnap, and return to the Exchange on Friday morning—probably in the same suit of clothes—without having to commute home.

For all of the adversity that brokers and investors alike had faced on Black Thursday, many survivors of this initial panic felt that the day had ended on an optimistic note, thanks to the organized bank support. What they didn't realize was that their ordeal was far from over. Over the next few days, the market would sputter into an irreversible decline, ushering in the Great Depression. Farmers, urbanites, professionals, and laborers would be dogged by years of hardship, the likes of which few could have imagined when much of America basked in postwar prosperity. Soon, the Roaring Twenties would become a distant whisper in the country's collective memory.

"Roaring Twenties" or Silent Depression?

2

"There were prophets of doom, but their warnings were drowned out by the wail of the saxophone and the ring of the cash register."
—author Stewart Ross, in *Causes and Consequences of the Great Depression*

How could the bottom fall out of the New York Stock Exchange as it did in October of 1929? Although people simply blamed rampant speculation, it is worthwhile to examine what motivated people to use the stock market as a get-rich-quick instrument during the 1920s. To understand the conditions leading up to the Crash, it is also important to keep in mind that stock prices reflect human emotion and intuition more than anything else.

A share of stock is worth whatever people are willing to pay for it; a very popular stock's inflated price often has little to do with the actual monetary value of the product or service it represents. This is in part because it is simply human nature for entire groups of people to believe something for no better reason than because they want it to be true. This human foible is nowhere more apparent than on the stock market, where people can convince themselves that they deserve to get rich quickly and without much effort if only they are clever enough to invest in the next hula hoop or handheld computer. For this reason, Wall Street stands out in popular mythology as a place where buttoned-down adventurers can make their dreams come true.

Wall Street is an eight-block street on the southern tip of Manhattan Island. It opens up to Trinity and Church Streets on Broadway to the west; it terminates at the East River to the east. In 1653, colonial Dutch settlers built a 12-foot high fence along the strip that would eventually become Wall Street. This fence was intended to keep livestock in—and British and Native American attackers out.

The first brokers began meeting under a button-wood tree on Wall Street to trade during the late 1700s. They dealt in Continentals, colonial bills with no coin money to back them up (thus, the old phrase, "not worth a Continental."). When people redeemed Continentals, they received certificates with a face value representing the sum that their paper money had been worth. These certificates were the first stocks and bonds.

On May 17, 1792, a group of 24 brokers made a formal agreement to deal with one another exclusively. That agreement marks the official birthday of the Exchange. By 1817 the brokers had outgrown their buttonwood tree, and the New York Stock and Exchange Board took up residence at 40 Wall Street. Known simply as the New York Stock Exchange since 1865, the trading floor moved twice before ending up at 18 Broad Street, just south of Wall Street. (Most people still speak of "Wall Street" when describing trading and brokerage activities in the vicinity of both Wall and Broad Streets, which is the hub of such activity in America.)

Stockbrokers do not sell goods or services; instead, they sell securities. Securities can be either bonds or stocks. In order to afford a physical plant, employees, raw materials, and appropriate training, companies need money, called capital. To gain capital, the company may invite people to invest their money in its bonds or stocks. People may buy bonds in a business if they wish to invest their money with relatively little risk. A bondholder in effect loans his or her money to

This painting depicts New York brokers meeting under a buttonwood tree on Wall Street in 1792. The modern stock market dates from May of that year, when 24 brokers agreed to deal exclusively with one another.

a business, receiving a certificate for the value of the money invested. When bondholders redeem their bonds, they make back the amount of money they originally paid, plus interest (a charge for borrowed money, generally a percentage of the amount borrowed) for the loan.

When people buy stock, on the other hand, they are actually buying partial ownership of the company in question. Stocks are sold in units called shares—one share usually equals one vote when a company's shareholders meet to make decisions. There are two ways to profit from stocks: investment and speculation. Investors hold on to their shares of stock for the long haul, making money when a company issues them a portion of its profits, called dividends. Stockholders may receive dividends from one to four times per year. Sometimes, however, instead of paying out dividends a company may elect to reinvest those profits into the company. The other way that people make money from stocks is called speculation. Unlike investors, speculators have no interest in keeping their stocks. Instead, they wait for prices to rise, then sell when they think that prices won't climb any higher. Speculation is the riskiest—and potentially most profitable—way to play the stock market.

Even though many novices tried their hands at stock market speculation during the 1920s, the practice was hardly new. This type of trading has been common in the stock market since before the American Revolution. The only necessary conditions for widespread speculation, according to John Kenneth Galbraith, are a euphoric sense of optimism, coupled with a mass willingness to believe that any given commodity is actually worth whatever people are willing to pay for it. That "given commodity" has at various times been land, gold—even tulip bulbs!

Amsterdam, capital of the Netherlands, boasted the first modern stock market as the term is known today. In the 1630s, tulip bulbs, with their promise of dazzling blooms in many colors, caught the public eye. Suddenly, people couldn't get enough of the bulbs and their prices soared. The Dutch took to buying tulip bulbs for outrageous sums, then waiting to sell them for still more money.

"Tulipomania" came to an unpretty end in 1637, when some of the buyers realized that the high prices couldn't last and rushed to sell. This triggered so many sales that tulip bulbs soon lost their wildly inflated value. People who had risked their property to invest in tulip bulbs suddenly found themselves displaced, without any means of raising enough money to buy back their homes. The impact of this seemingly funny Dutch obsession with tulips was anything but humorous. Holland was mired in an economic depression after the speculative bubble burst.

During the 1920s, it was not Dutch tulips, but Florida real estate that everybody wanted. The practice of buying land in Florida with as little as 10 percent down became very popular from 1924 to 1926. Buyers often didn't bother to inspect their purchases and the fact that much of the "beachfront" property changing hands was actually swampland mattered little. After all, the landowners weren't planning to build on the tiny (sometimes as small as 1/23 of an acre) lots, which were increasing in value despite their shortcomings. Instead, they planned to sell to the highest bidder—just as soon as it dawned on the very rich that a villa in the Sunshine State was a necessity. What speculators overlooked was that eventually people would realize that slivers of impossible-to-develop land were not worth buying.

In the first half of 1926, the parade of buyers started thinning out. Florida land prices soon plummeted, leaving those who had bought on credit wiped out.

The Florida land boom and bust should have sounded a warning bell in the ears of many Americans about the hazards of speculation. But people burned by the real estate bust ultimately blamed two hurricanes that struck Florida—one of which killed some 400 people on September 18, 1926—for their misfortune, rather than their risky real-estate speculation.

But who could blame ordinary people for getting caught up in the quest for wealth? They were trying to make good on their share of the unbridled optimism that characterized the 1920s following the First World War. Although the United States had suffered casualties in the war, they were relatively limited when compared with the loss of life suffered in Europe. Unlike the European countries, America's geography was unscathed by the ravages of battle. And the war effort had led to increased production and employment, as people hustled to build things like ships and weapons. Even after the soldiers returned to reclaim their jobs, production levels remained high.

The number of construction starts and the rate of steel production were just two of the indicators that people used to judge the nation's overall prosperity. The steel industry was robust until 1929, but the number of new homes being constructed had begun declining earlier in the 1920s. Yet this trend caused little

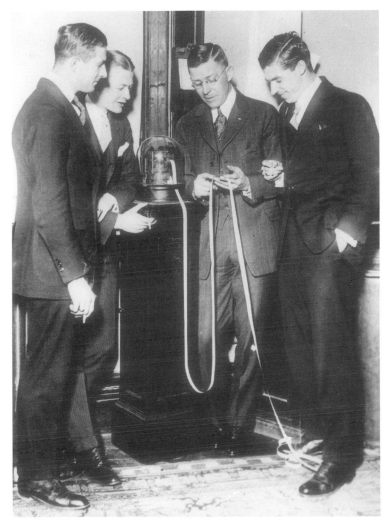

Four brokers read stock quotations on a ticker-tape machine, a piece of equipment that received information over telegraph lines and reprinted it on a tape ribbon. This photo was taken in 1923, when John Borg, the 42-year-old man holding the tape, announced that he had made enough money in the stock market—$2 million—and was going to retire. He gave his brokerage business to the three employees standing around him. It was success stories like this one that encouraged many people to speculate in the stock market during the 1920s.

alarm at the time, especially in light of the good news on the automotive front. Over 4 million new cars rolled off American assembly lines in 1926. That number would increase to over 5 million in 1929.

A new way of buying things helped people come up with the $500 or so that it cost to buy a new family-sized car. Many Americans discovered the joys of credit, which also allowed them to afford radios, sewing machines, and even houses. As Americans emerged from World War I secure in the knowledge that they lived in the most powerful and prosperous nation on earth, they grew increasingly willing to use credit to have the things they wanted immediately. The economy seemed strong, so people were confident that they could buy now and pay later.

There were subtle clues that all was not well on the economic horizon, but few people noticed them or interpreted these signs as dark omens. While the demand for modern convenience items for sale increased steadily, most people's wages remained about the same. More Americans than ever before could be considered very rich during the 1920s, but it was mostly the rich who were getting richer. The disparity between rich and poor was so dramatic that Galbraith estimated that the wealthiest 5 percent of Americans made about one-third of all of the income generated in 1929. In another book, *The Stock Market Crash of 1929,* author Nancy Millichap stated that 20 percent of all Americans made more than 50 percent of all American money. This uneven distribution of money became an important factor in the stock market crash, because it was the rich who financed most of the activity on Wall Street. As they panicked and withdrew their money in 1929, the market was doomed to free-fall.

In the midst of the so-called "Roaring Twenties," however, the comfortably well off did not notice the increasingly unbalanced economy. Radio and print advertisements urged people to spend on everything from cigars to women's facial soap, and they did. Even if they were not truly rich, people aspired to attain the appearance of wealth. The sky seemed to be the limit.

People occasionally crossed legal boundaries in order to chase wealth. Since the Eighteenth Amendment and the Volstead Act had outlawed the production, sale, and transportation of alcoholic beverages in 1919, some Americans felt grudging admiration for the reckless organized crime figures who grew rich by producing "bathtub gin" and opening illegal bars, called "speakeasies." Even proper-looking young women were among those who hid liquor in the backs of their cars, transporting it to the shadowy speakeasies frequented by many other ordinarily law-abiding citizens.

However, even in this age of unparalleled national confidence, there were many who could only dream of effortless prosperity. Approximately one-third of all Americans participated in some type of farming to support themselves during the 1920s. These family farmers had profited from the misfortune of European farmers during World War I. The war years and those immediately thereafter were agriculturally unproductive in Europe, where devastation and death had left many farmers incapable of scraping together what remained of their crops and herds. The U.S. government sent the European countries relief to bridge the gap, resulting in robust demand for American farm products. But this demand dropped as European agriculture recovered from the ravages of war. From 1925 to 1929, American farmers watched prices for their wares plummet 30 percent. They were left holding a surplus of crops, meat, and eggs, and barely hanging on financially.

But many others felt sufficiently insulated from the plight of the family farmer to dream of eventual

"Shall we be more tender with our dollars than with the Lives of our sons"

W.G. McAdoo
Secretary of the Treasury

Buy a United States Government Bond of the

2nd LIBERTY LOAN
of 1917

No.1

During World War I, the government sold "Liberty Bonds" to help finance the U.S. war effort. As people began to earn a return on their bond investments, they became interested in investing money in stocks as well.

wealth. The time seemed right even for those who had never before considered it to try their luck on the stock market. People had become comfortable investing their money during World War I when they purchased Liberty Bonds. These bonds were promissory notes issued by the United States government, guaranteeing a payback of the investor's loan, plus interest, after a given number of years. Silent film stars like Mary Pickford had urged all Americans to purchase Liberty Bonds in order to help support the war effort.

The popularity of Liberty Bonds probably encouraged people to investigate other ways of making their money work for them. These eager novice investors were as a group unwilling to endure the slow and steady climb that long-term investment entails; they wanted to speculate, to buy the right stock and sell it as soon as its price peaked. In their zeal to get more for less, Americans favored common stocks over preferred stocks.

Both common and preferred stocks represent ownership in a corporation. As the name suggests, there are advantages to owning preferred stock. In the 1920s, preferred stocks were more expensive per share, but shareholders were guaranteed dividends. A common stockholder, on the other hand, had no such guarantee but the stock cost less per share. The lower price of common stock is only one explanation for its popularity during the 1920s, however. Preferred stock was generally less subject to rapid drops in price, but its gains were also more limited. Common stock was relatively mercurial in nature, but this instability held the promise of a dramatic rise in price if investors were lucky enough to anticipate the next hot commodity.

During the 1920s bull market, stockbrokers turned their attention to small investors as never before. Stockbrokers advertised their services as a way to help the average person get rich. Even those without the money to pay for stock up front could join in on the speculation game. Thanks to margin accounts, investors could buy shares of stock from their brokers for as little as 10 percent of the actual price. The broker would get a loan (called a broker's loan) from a bank to pay for the balance of the stock's price. He or she would purchase the stock for the investor, using the stock itself as collateral. If everything went as the investor hoped, he or she could make enough to cover the loan plus the margin deposit, and then pocket the leftover profit.

For example, if Investor X bought a share of stock for $100 with 10 percent down, the broker would secure a bank loan for the remaining $90 and then buy the stock. If the stock shot up to $165 a share, prompting Investor X to sell, he or she would recover the initial $10 investment, pay back the $90 margin account and perhaps an additional $10 for interest on the loan and broker's fees, leaving Investor X with $55 of pure profit. The broker, in turn, would pay back the broker's loan of $90, plus interest, and pocket his share of the fees.

But if Investor X made an unfortunate choice of stock to purchase, he or she would get a margin call from the broker once the stock's price dipped below the total amount loaned (below $90 per share in this example). A margin call is a telephone call or telegram ordering an investor to place more cash into his or her margin account in order to keep the stock. If the investor cannot come up with enough money, the broker sells off the stock. The broker then uses the proceeds of that sale to repay the broker's loan to the bank. The hapless investor is left with nothing—or worse, becomes indebted to his or her broker if the sale of the stock doesn't cover the margin account.

While it is true that many people did get rich through speculation, at least as many met with financial ruin. Some people got rich once, then reinvested their money in further speculative ventures only to get wiped out on their second try! The stories of the stock market in the 1920s were just as unique as the individuals who tried their luck.

In the minds of many, the economic climate of 1920s America was one of unlimited promise. Those who emerged victorious from the speculation game were revered as financial wizards—regardless of whether it was wits or blind luck that had brought them wealth. Stock prices in the 1920s were—as they still are—a reflection of an entire people's mental state, rather than an expression of any one commodity's intrinsic value. With the First World War a fading memory and employment high, stock prices soared with few fluctuations from 1924 to 1929.

The seemingly unstoppable bull market of the

Roaring Twenties led some economists to grandly proclaim that financial crashes and panics were a thing of the past. With the clarity that comes with hindsight, many historians have since theorized that a "silent depression" was actually weakening the economy so much that the eventual Crash was destined to become the proverbial last straw. The slump in home building, the extension of credit despite stagnant wages, and the uneven distribution of wealth were a few signs of trouble lurking beneath the opulent surface. Another was America's postwar status as a creditor nation: some smaller countries could not repay loans made by American banks. Peru, for example, defaulted on over $90 million in loans from the securities branch of New York's National City Bank.

Then there were the destabilizing forces within the stock market itself. The New York Stock Exchange of the 1920s saw price manipulations that made an illustrious few magnificently wealthy at the expense of many small investors. These major players frequently got richer on the backs of unsuspecting small investors. Ironically, average investors dreamed of joining the ranks of the very people who were exploiting their desire for wealth.

Bulls, Bears, Price Manipulations, and Panics

3

B y 1929 there were 1,375 "seated" brokers who were licensed to trade on the New York Stock Exchange floor; each of them had shelled out $600,000 for the privilege. The prohibitive cost of a seat on the Exchange meant that only wealthy individuals or the floor brokers of the most preeminent companies could afford to be there. This exclusivity fostered a clubby atmosphere that turned a blind eye to some unsavory insider trading practices. These tricks of the trade often worked to the detriment of small investors.

Price manipulations and dubious financial practices came in a variety of forms in the 1920s—just as they do today. Even the titans of the New York Stock exchange who used big money to make more money often fell to ruin. But for every big investor wiped out on Wall Street, countless smaller ones paid the price for large-scale schemes gone awry. They lacked the advantage of "inside" information that could save them from losing their money. The movements of the market often caught them especially unaware.

As in any business, there are numerous tactics employed in an effort to reach the same goal. In the Exchange, that goal is of course to maximize profit. The surging stock market encouraged bulls (people who anticipate a continued rise in stock prices) to speculate. But some shrewd bears (people who purchase stock with the expectation that its price will drop) also made out very well by ferreting out unstable stocks, and then selling them short.

Short selling is especially risky because it entails selling borrowed stocks. If a bearish trader suspects that a given stock's price is about to fall, he or she borrows shares of that stock from a broker, then sells them as quickly as possible. If all goes according to plan, the trader waits until the stock's price has dropped to its lowest expected point. Then the "bear" buys back the shares at this drastically reduced price. After returning the borrowed shares to the broker, the successful short seller pockets the difference between the proceeds of the first sale and the reduced buy-back price.

The best short sellers put an extra flourish on their craft called "covering." Short sellers who cover convince other investors to sell their stock, too, so that they can buy huge blocks of it for themselves. Once the price drops, the person who initiated the wave of selling then buys back the stock sold by others in addition to his or her own. Traders who are smooth enough to pull off covering in addition to short selling can get a "corner" on the stock of their choice (ownership and control over a large enough portion of a given stock to influence its price) at minimal expense to themselves.

Jesse Livermore was one of Wall Street's most famous short sellers in the 1920s. A middle-aged man with a taste for well-made suits and expensive cigars, Livermore had an inscrutable manner and a knack for sensing which stocks were about to falter. He was also influential in "bulling up," or increasing, stock prices: Livermore was the main force behind the rise of the stock prices of the food market chain Piggly Wiggly in 1920. He also joined the famous Durant consortium of over 20 millionaires who pooled, or combined, their money to drive up stock prices. (For all of his uncanny instincts, however, Jesse Livermore was no match for the Stock Market Crash of 1929. He lost everything.)

William "Billy" Durant was perhaps the best-known protagonist of the pooling dramas that played out on Wall Street in the 1920s. He took part in a huge pooling syndicate that strongly influenced the New York Stock Exchange from 1924 to the spring of 1929. Pooling was a common, straightforward form of stock price manipulation during the 1920s. A group of investors would combine its money and one broker

Famous stock trader Jesse Livermore had grown wealthy during the money panic of 1907. He was known for "short selling" stocks, but could also drive up stock prices, if that was to his benefit.

would use the funds to buy up numerous shares of a particular stock on behalf of the group. The goal was to increase the price of that stock with a surge of buying. The pool relied on its collective buying power to induce other people to buy the stock. When pooling went the way it was supposed to, a stock's price soared.

Many of the investors who joined pools were financial heavy hitters who had made (and lost) fortunes on the stock market several times over. Pooling was not illegal, and it was hard to keep the practice a secret, since some of the brightest financial stars of 1920s Wall Street were involved. Their word was often enough to entice novice investors to buy a given stock, but it was hard for beginners to know when to sell. The pool members would sit on the shares they had purchased until they all agreed that prices had peaked. Then, they would begin selling the shares back onto the market at a gradual pace so as not to trigger a panic of selling that would make the price tumble abruptly. Selling off massive amounts of stock at a good price and without alarming smaller investors required intuition and skill.

Another tactic for artificially increasing a stock's price is called the "washed sale." A group of brokers agrees in advance to sell a given stock back and forth among themselves. The resulting surge of market activity creates the impression that the stock is attracting widespread interest. This illusory interest attracts other investors anxious to be in on a hot prospect. Their increased buying bulls up the price of the stock in question—allowing the brokers involved in the washed sale to sell it off at an inflated price.

Holding companies and investment trusts are not methods for price manipulation, but they are worth discussing. Like inside traders, business owners who create holding companies are trying to attract new investors. Holding companies are business entities that neither produce goods nor offer services. Instead, they exist solely to manage the securities and assets of another company. Since utility companies could legally issue only so many shares of common stock, for instance, holding companies took over utilities so that people could legally buy stock in the established company by buying stock in the new one. The money invested in these holding companies helped the owners of their parent companies dodge certain taxes, and the additional capital that the holding companies accumulated enabled their owners to buy out other companies. This led to centralized management of power companies.

One hazard of holding companies was that individuals could use them as leverage to build fundamentally unsound business empires. In theory, one holding company could control the stock of another holding company, which would in turn control other holding companies—which might then finally control the company that operated the actual business.

An aggressive businessman named Samuel Insull snapped up control of 65 utility companies, using a network of holding companies to finance his venture. When the Crash came in 1929, Insull promised his employees that he would shield them from personal ruin by securing their margin accounts. The truth was that he could not even save himself, and by the end of 1931 his empire fell apart. Insull threw himself under a Paris subway train while in hiding there.

Like many of his employees, Insull was an overextended speculator when the Crash caught up with him. But his instrument of speculation was investors' money, rather than brokers' loans. He got it fraudulently by issuing many more stocks than his companies were actually worth. Insull would then use this ill-gotten leverage to finance the takeover of still more utilities. Holding companies had allowed Samuel Insull to own many more utility companies than he could have actually paid for out of his own pocket. With the Crash came exposure of his crooked business practices and a tidal wave of financial ruin. Countless small investors in Insull's holding companies also lost their money.

With so many forces at work on the New York Stock Exchange, it may seem like panics and crashes should be annual events. Two elements of past financial panics were a weak, decentralized banking system and unchecked stock market speculation. Throughout history, those affected by these money panics have blamed earthquakes, hurricanes, and other unavoidable disasters for touching off crashes. While the economy does shudder when disasters destroy communities and natural resources, speculation is nearly always part of the scenario that leads to a crash. Another important component of money panics and crashes is just what the terminology indicates: panic. Frightened investors and depositors sell off their stocks or withdraw their money from banks en masse, weakening both the stock market and the banking system.

Wall Street experienced its first "Black Friday" on September 24, 1869. The medium of speculation behind this panic was not stock, but gold. Trading in gold was forbidden on the New York Stock Exchange, yet the collapse of gold prices at nearby Broad Street and Exchange Place plunged the stock market into a dramatic money panic.

In 1869, financier Jay Gould formed a syndicate to bull up the price of gold over at Broad Street and Exchange Place. He quietly snapped up over $100 million worth of gold certificates. Gould had chosen an opportune time to try cornering the gold market. American farmers had produced a crop surplus that year. To insure a good export price, they urged the national treasury to withhold all gold for commercial sale, which would keep gold prices strong overseas. Gould and his associates, Jim Fisk and Abel Corbin (who also happened to be President Ulysses S. Grant's brother-in-law,

Samuel Insull, photographed while awaiting trial after the collapse of his vast utilities holdings. Insull committed suicide before he could be convicted and jailed.

having married his sister Jennie) conspired to corner the entire supply of gold that was still commercially available. They looked forward to having the power to name their price for gold if the National Treasury did decide to withhold its store of gold from the market.

While Gould, Fisk, and Corbin were buying gold certificates, they were also trying to persuade President Grant to refrain from selling gold through the National Treasury. Gould argued that paper money was over-valued. He maintained that by withholding gold from the market, Grant could help adjust paper money's value to a more realistic level. The president seemed oblivious to Gould's ulterior motive—even when he found himself and his family seated at Fisk's Manhattan theater for a special evening of entertainment with Gould, Fisk, and Corbin as his hosts!

It was one thing to wine and dine President Grant, but by September the Gould syndicate wanted him out of the way while it completed its assault on the gold market. Corbin helpfully suggested that his brother-in-law visit an old friend in a rural Pennsylvania town that just happened to have no telegraph station. On September 13, Grant was on his way to the country for some rest and relaxation. With the president conveniently stashed in the middle of nowhere, the Gould group bought up gold certificates with renewed vigor.

Unbeknownst to Gould, however, President Grant was growing suspicious. He urged his wife to write Jennie Corbin in New York City, to inform both Corbins that he was "very much disturbed" by the Gould syndicate's speculation in gold. Once Jay Gould learned that the jig was up, he elected to withhold this information from James Fisk. He let his coconspirator continue the buying frenzy, but he began to gradually sell off his gold. By this time, the price of gold was up to $150. (It took $150 worth of paper money to purchase $100 worth of gold certificates, which were redeemable for the real thing.)

The drama of the gold frenzy may have been playing itself out in the "gold room" at Broad Street and Exchange Place, but its impact was being felt just as keenly on the New York Stock Exchange floor. Speculation in gold had become so popular that investors were redirecting the money they would ordinarily have spent on stocks into gold certificates. Wall

Street's money was literally drying up.

The situation came to a head on Friday, September 24. By 11:00 A.M., gold prices had peaked at $164. But President Grant was back in Washington and ready to clamp down on gold speculation. He announced that, effective noon the next day, the Treasury would make $4 million in gold available for sale. The Treasury would also buy $4 million in bonds at that time.

The news immediately sent Broad Street and Exchange Place's gold room reeling—even though a mere $4 million worth of government gold was not really enough to turn the economic tide. Grant's announcement had, however, sent the unmistakable message that gold prices were artificially high and poised to tumble.

As gold prices slid downhill for the rest of Black Friday, Jay Gould huddled in an associate's nearby office. A tempest of panic and disillusionment swept through the gold room. When he was ready to leave his hiding place, law enforcement officials had to prevent angry investors from clobbering him. James Fisk also barely escaped in one piece. Gould and his cronies ultimately incurred losses of about $50 million. The syndicate's broker, William Belden, lost his bankrupt brokerage house as a result of the crash.

Numerous investors who had bought gold on credit lost incalculable amounts of money. But it is human nature to quickly forget the lessons learned in a financial crisis. Within a few short decades of a crash, panic, or depression, people eagerly jumped back into the sport of speculation with high hopes of striking it rich. After Black Friday of 1869 came the Money Panic of 1907. More than any other event on Wall Street

A nervous crowd lines up on October 23, 1907, to withdraw money from the Colonial Deposit Company at Ann Street and Broadway in New York. Many banks, both large and small, failed during the Money Panic of 1907.

leading up to the Crash of 1929, the events of 1907 were an omen of things to come.

On April 18, 1906, a powerful earthquake and the three days of fire that followed it destroyed half of San Francisco. The loss of industry and employment in the area—coupled with the huge payouts that insurance companies had to put into rebuilding the city—had taken a toll on America's money supply by 1907. Stock prices, which are an index of people's overall confidence in business, faltered.

However, the San Francisco earthquake was just one factor in the 1907 panic. The earthquake created a backdrop of weakness that made the market more vulnerable to running out of cash. The nation's weak banking system was another factor in the Money Panic of 1907. As panicked depositors responded to the dip in stock prices by withdrawing their cash from banks, the banks started to run out of money. Many banks had made themselves even more vulnerable to collapse by funding stock market speculation too liberally. Although this practice was illegal in many states, banks had circumvented the laws by setting up satellite investment companies that did the actual lending.

Although small local banks were especially vulnerable, big New York City banks were also susceptible to "bank runs"—mass withdrawals that wiped out their cash. A notable example was Heinze's Mercantile National Bank, a large and highly regarded New York City institution. In the fall of 1907, word spread that Heinze's was short on cash because of its involvement in heavy speculation in a weak stock market. When the Knickerbocker Trust Company, a fixture on Fifth Avenue, also started running out of money, the panic grew. Investors found out about the Knickerbocker's troubles because the bank's directors were foolish enough to discuss the problem in a fashionable New York restaurant where people could easily eavesdrop on the meeting.

A full-scale bank panic struck. On Tuesday, October 22, the Knickerbocker closed down within a mere two-and-a-half hours of opening. Bank tellers tried to stall the throngs of people anxious to retrieve their cash by closing down to one booth for withdrawals, "accidentally" spilling change, and checking everything twice. Customers had a few tricks of their own, too. Some would go the deposit windows—where there

Charles H. Dow and Edward T. Jones founded Dow Jones and Company, which began publishing the *Wall Street Journal* in 1889. For more than a century, the Dow-Jones Industrial Average has been the most recognized measure of stock values.

were no lines—and put tiny amounts of cash into their accounts, then make large withdrawals while they had a teller's attention. At Knickerbocker Trust Company and countless other banks, many depositors camped overnight to keep their positions in line, hoping to reach the tellers' windows before the cash ran out. Some enterprising youngsters would wait in line, then sell their positions at the front for a few dollars.

In their panic, New Yorkers looked for someone who could reverse the tumbling stock prices. The venerable founder of J. P. Morgan and Company seemed a likely candidate. That Morgan was 70 years old and enfeebled by a case of the flu mattered little to a man like Oakley Thorne. Thorne was the chairman of the Trust Company of America, the latest big New York City bank to falter. He pleaded for Morgan's help. Morgan, who had been meeting with leading city bankers at his library for several days, called them into a decisive gathering on October 24.

This meeting took place in the nick of time. At 1 P.M., New York Stock Exchange president Ransome H. Thomas informed Morgan that cash for trading securities had dried up. Unless something was done to infuse money into the Exchange, its shutdown was imminent. In less than half an hour, Morgan and the bankers secured $27 million to save the Trust Company of America and revitalize the stock market.

Conditions at the Exchange floor improved almost as soon as word of Morgan's emergency funding reached the floor. But completely reversing the downhill slide on stock prices took several weeks. Before the panic was over, the Morgan group would funnel a total of over $40 million into New York's banks. The elderly Morgan's role in stemming the Money Panic of 1907 elevated him to folk-hero status in the minds of many people. But the financial icon did not act alone; Secretary of the Treasury George Cortelyou directed some $250 million of government money into the banking system to save failing banks and discourage bank runs.

To many people who lived through the Money Panic of 1907, the crisis seemed to have come on suddenly, touched off by the San Francisco earthquake. But the quake was just one factor that stressed an already overextended banking system to the breaking point. By the time 1929 rolled around, the Money Panic of 1907 was a dim memory. The stock market was hurtling skyward, and people were gambling for their piece of the American Dream. Laborers and little old ladies with margin accounts were playing the market alongside legendary bulls and bears. Market-watchers breathlessly tracked the ascending Dow-Jones Industrial Average. (Developed by Charles H. Dow in 1896 as a 12-stock price index, since 1928 the Dow-Jones Industrial Average has indicated the stock prices for 30 leading companies listed on the New York Stock Exchange.) Nobody wanted to hear even the slightest murmuring of trouble ahead.

Trouble Ahead?

In 1929 the economy was headed for trouble. Eventually that trouble was
violently reflected in Wall Street.
—John Kenneth Galbraith, *The Great Crash of 1929*

Although stock prices blazed skyward for most of 1929, a regulatory banking agency called the Federal Reserve Board was
growing increasingly anxious about the unfettered speculation
that helped fuel the Big Bull market.

The Federal Reserve Board had been formed in 1913 to regulate the
amount of money available in the U.S. banking system at any given
time. From its headquarters in Washington, D.C., the board oversaw 12

New York bank director Charles E. Mitchell's stand against the Federal Reserve Board in the spring of 1929 helped prevent a bank panic.

district Federal Reserve Banks across the country. These banks would loan money to smaller member banks in their respective districts.

Early in 1929, the directors of the Federal Reserve Bank of New York wanted to raise the rediscount rate on loans to member banks. This is the interest rate charged by the Federal Reserve Board on monies borrowed by banks. The Board knew that banks were borrowing from the Federal Reserve to finance broker's loans. To deter banks from doing this, New York reserve bank officials wanted to make money "tighter" with an increased interest rate, even though they knew that any measure to deter speculation would be unpopular.

On February 14, 1929, the New York Federal Reserve Bank suggested that the rediscount rate be raised from 5 to 6 percent. But the Federal Reserve Board in Washington refused. The board knew that people would interpret an increased rediscount rate as a sign that the bull market was headed for a crash. This interpretation would then become a self-fulfilling prophecy, as investors swamped the New York Stock Exchange with sell orders and pulled their money from banks. The Federal Reserve Board did, however, issue letters to its 12 district banks telling them to curb loans for speculative purposes to member banks.

On March 4, Herbert Hoover began his presidency. Soon after, the Federal Reserve Board began holding daily meetings behind closed doors. The board members did not talk about the purpose of these meetings, so people assumed the worst. A mini-panic ensued on Wall Street. On March 26, investors sold off stocks, causing prices to fall by as much as 30 points. As more and more people sold, brokers sent telegrams to clients requesting additional cash to maintain their margin accounts. Some investors who could not come up with the money found themselves deeply indebted to their brokers by the end of the day.

Banks around the country had responded to the Federal Reserve Board's secrecy by raising their interest rates on broker's loans. One notable exception was National City Bank, headed by Charles Mitchell—who also happened to be a director of the New York Federal Reserve Bank. Mitchell issued a bold statement during the March 26 panic in which he promised that National City would not raise its interest rates on broker's loans. He stood up to the ominously silent Federal Reserve Board because he felt strongly that it should step aside, keep money "loose," and let the bull market continue unimpeded.

Emboldened by the example of National City Bank, many other banks decided to flout the Federal Reserve Board, too. They kept their interest rates on brokers' loans at their present level. Mitchell's stand against the "Fed" restored confidence in the banking system; the panic began and ended on March 26. "The Federal Reserve remained silent," wrote John Kenneth

Galbraith, "but now its silence was reassuring. It meant that it conceded Mitchell's mastery."

Not everyone was for letting the boom continue unfettered. But anyone who urged more moderation on Wall Street instantly became unpopular. When Paul Warburg, one of the Federal Reserve Board's original members, warned in March that the country was headed for a depression if unchecked stock market speculation continued, his remarks were met with hostility from other market-watchers.

Others were not content to simply disagree with those who wanted the bull market to be kept more firmly in hand. They went directly to the White House, urging the president to call off the Federal Reserve Board at once. William Durant allegedly paid a nighttime visit to President Hoover on April 4. Durant supposedly warned the president that unless the Federal Reserve Board stopped trying to control speculation by limiting the amount of money available for margin accounts, the New York Stock Exchange was headed for a devastating crash. The story of Durant's pitch to the president also includes the results of a rather unscientific poll he conducted in which he had asked 100 prominent executives if they believed their companies' stock prices to be artificially high. He is said to have then presented the commander in chief with the resulting deluge of "no" answers as proof that the stock market needed to keep charging upward without government interference.

Nobody disputes the fact that months later, Thomas Lamont, J. P. Morgan and Company's top man, tried to give President Hoover a similar message. Lamont chose a more scholarly approach than Durant did, however.

He sent Hoover a 20-page report refuting the necessity of "corrective action on the part of public authorities or individuals" that would interfere with what he deemed America's "brilliant" financial future.

Indeed, the summer of 1929 had given Thomas Lamont and everyone else so inclined ample reason to believe in the possibility of a never-ending bull market. In August, the Federal Reserve Board finally raised the rediscount rate from 5 to 6 percent. The panic that the Board had feared igniting months earlier never materialized. On August 20, the Dow-Jones Industrial Average hit an all-time high of 331 points. Just two weeks later, the stock market broke that record. On September 3, the New York Stock Exchange reached a Dow-Jones average of 381 (although the highest pre-crash *closing* average—the average at the end of a day of trading—on the NYSE was 353 points, reached on October 10, 1929). With the exchange of 4,438,910 shares of stock, September 3 was the most active day of trading recorded to that point.

Brokers and investors had scarcely caught their collective breath after that whirlwind day when a note of caution filled the air. On Thursday, September 5, economist Roger Babson addressed the National Business Conference, which was held in Boston. He predicted an imminent crash that would cause the currently soaring Dow-Jones to tumble a whopping 60 to 80 points. This grim prognostication alone was enough to send shock waves through Wall Street. Stock prices dipped almost immediately. But once the initial scare subsided, the drop in prices also halted. Babson's prediction was either ignored or ridiculed by other well-known economists for causing what they saw as groundless fear.

Investors preferred to listen to economists like Irving Fisher (left), who in mid-October 1929 predicted that stock prices had reached "a permanantly high plateau"; few heeded Roger Babson's September warning: "Sooner or later a crash is coming."

As summer gave way to fall, anyone looking for signs of trouble could have marshaled a fairly ominous body of evidence. Stock prices were still high, but other indices of America's economic confidence and health were falling. Rates of construction starts, automobile and steel production, and employment were all declining. Hardly anyone wanted to look for potential problems, though. It was as if Americans were too captivated by the charge of the bull market to believe that prices would ever retreat.

Roger Babson's September 5 warning may not have started a money panic, but it did herald the unofficial end of the Roaring Twenties. Nobody seemed to realize it at the time, though. From the week of Babson's statement until the Great Crash, stock prices started on an insidious downward trend. The slide was so gradual that expert economists and amateur speculators alike attributed it to a "technical correction." They reasoned that if they could just ride out a short spell of faltering stock prices, they would reap the rewards of their staying power once the market shook out the weakest investors and resumed its bullish stampede upward.

Even the Federal Reserve Board's August decision to increase its rediscount rate had failed to raise many people's eyebrows. Although plenty of banks responded by raising their interest rates on loans to brokers, the market hardly missed a beat. Charles Mitchell barely acknowledged the Fed's decision, again refusing to raise National City Bank's interest rates on brokers' loans. The Morgan banking house kept its interest rates down, too. These big New York banks reasoned that their willingness to offer low-interest brokers' loans would help sustain the bull market by keeping margin accounts readily available. But by encouraging speculation, they also encouraged more people to place themselves in financial peril by over-extending themselves with margin accounts they couldn't possibly repay if the market collapsed. Banks that did not raise their interest rates increased their risk of running out of cash if too many margin account holders defaulted on their debts to brokers.

Stock prices continued their slow fizzle into October. A few New York newspapers intimated that perhaps the bull market wasn't destined to last. Yet people still preferred to hear the glowing reports from people like Irving Fisher (who predicted, "Stock prices have reached what looks like a permanently high plateau.") and Charles Mitchell (who pronounced the condition of America's businesses "absolutely sound"). Both men made these statements on October 15.

Some Americans practiced a sort of willful obliviousness to bad news about the stock market, while others truly were taken completely by surprise when the Crash came. But it is also true that many more were oblivious to what was happening on Wall Street because they had no involvement with it whatsoever.

We associate the Roaring Twenties so closely with fast-and-loose stock market speculation that it is easy to overlook the fact that only a minority of the population was involved in it. John Kenneth Galbraith writes that "only one and a half million people, out of a population of approximately 120 million and of between 29 and 30 million families, had an active association of any sort with the stock market." He also points out that the majority of investors did not trade on margin. But a striking feature of trading on margin during the 1920s bull market was that it had become a fad among middle-class investors. Even though the popular notion that everyone was playing the market was false, a huge number of people did try it for the first time during the so-called Big Bull Market. This meant that talk of the market and hot stocks permeated the popular culture at dinner parties and on the street as never before and became a permanent part of the lore of the Roaring Twenties.

The impact of the losses incurred by this new breed of investor is not to be minimized, however. Although their number was smaller than one might suppose, the investors were still a significant minority—especially once the Crash left many of them ruined. Moreover, the Great Depression that followed the Crash did not discriminate between those who had been involved in the market and the majority of Americans who hadn't.

But those middle-class Americans who were still holding their shares in October of 1929 had no inkling of what was to come. Most still looked hopefully to the future for an improvement in stock market conditions. If small-time investors had ever resented the Wall Street insiders who grew richer through such subterfuges as pools and washed sales, it was hard to tell now. People spoke of pooling in positive terms. Instead of disparaging talk about "syndicates," there came hopeful gossip about the possibility of "organized support" shoring up prices. Many waited anxiously for Wall Street's heavy hitters to charge onto the Exchange floor and buy up millions of shares in an effort to revive the arrested bull market.

By the time people started hoping for "organized support," however, it was already too late. The stage for the Great Crash had been slowly setting itself throughout the high-living Twenties. But many Americans were still giddy enough from their ride on the Big Bull Market to believe that things were sure to improve. They held on till the end—which was soon to come.

Black Days

Police had to be called to control the crowd that gathered outside the New York Stock Exchange on October 24.

Monday, October 21, saw an anxious wave of selling on the New York Stock Exchange. In addition to those who sold voluntarily, there were many margin account holders who could not avoid having their stocks sold out from under them. The ticker tape—that slip of paper upon which investors' next moves were predicated—could not keep up with the actual rate of selling. Although trading closed at 3:00 P.M., the day's last readings did not come in until after 4:40 P.M. Over six million shares were traded; some unnecessarily, as it turned out. Jittery shareholders decided to sell because they saw the stock prices taking a nosedive. Because every ticker in the nation fell so far behind, however, they could only act on a very limited vision of the future. They sold—or their brokers sold them out—because nobody could predict just how bad things would get on the basis of less-than-current ticker tape readings. But back at the NYSE, prices actually rallied during the last hour of trading. This recovery was no consolation for many investors, though. By the time the final ticker readings came in with the "good" news, it was too late for them to recoup the loss of their personal fortunes.

Tuesday, October 22, brought more of the same, except that prices failed to rebound at the end of the day. They did climb a little after the Exchange opened for trading at 10:00 A.M., only to drop for the remainder of the session until the 3:00 P.M. close. Stock prices were down by an average of 50 points from their September 3 pinnacle.

Despite mounting evidence to the contrary, some acknowledged experts continued to preach optimism. Yale economist Irving Fisher espoused the theory of technical correction. On October 21, he had characterized the stock market's ills as a "shaking out of the lunatic fringe." Fisher meant that the most unstable, insolvent speculators were being weeded out of the market. The survivors of the slump, he felt, would be able to bull stock prices back up to their former levels.

October 23 on the Exchange floor was characterized by an uninterrupted drop in prices. The ticker fell a staggering 104 minutes behind actual transactions as selling heated up in response to sliding stock prices.

Even against this worrisome backdrop, a few steadfast bulls were busy forming pools in the hope of injecting new life into the market. But many more people were finally beginning to sense that the Big Bull

Market was irretrievably gone. Rumors of sold-out investors and ruined brokers leaping into the East River and out of tall buildings began circulating around New York City. Although the gossip ultimately proved to be exaggerated, some city papers ran out of reporters to follow all the tips of suicides that poured into their offices.

The market performed so dismally on October 24 that the day became known as "Black Thursday." Hopeful talk of "organized support" was in the air before the opening bell rang on the NYSE trading floor. The gossip ultimately became fact, but not before the situation grew truly desperate.

All morning, *air pockets* permeated the stock mar-

These Wall Street clerks and brokers were among the hundreds who worked for 48 straight hours processing the incredible volume of stock transactions made on October 24th and 25th.

ket. These occurred when nobody would come forward to buy a given stock at any price. Even normally vigorous stocks like U.S. Steel and General Motors experienced them on October 24. The New York Stock Exchange was flying apart before the very eyes of the spectators in its visitors' gallery. The gallery was closed by 12:30 P.M. in an attempt to hide the disarray on the trading floor behind closed doors. The people who vacated the gallery poured into the crowd already gathered on Wall Street.

Just a short walk away, a historic meeting was taking place. Although J. P. Morgan was long dead, his banking house was reprising the role it had taken in stopping the 1907 panic. Thomas Lamont, J. P. Morgan and Company's top spokesman, was playing host this time at the Morgan offices at 23 Wall Street. Attending this meeting to address the money crisis on the Exchange were Charles Mitchell, chair of National City Bank; William Potter, head of Guaranty Trust Company; Albert Wiggin of Chase National Bank; and Seward Prosser, head of Bankers Trust Company. Just as the consortium of New York bankers had done at Morgan's Park Avenue home 22 years earlier, this group pondered the "hows and whys" of emergency funding for the Exchange.

As was the case in 1907, self-preservation motivated these bankers to consider bailing out the New York Stock Exchange. If the Exchange closed for the day with stocks at their current dismal prices, brokerage houses would be left unable to repay banks for their loans on sold-out margin accounts. Conditions would then be ripe for widespread, devastating bank runs by frightened depositors.

As far as the big New York City banks were concerned, the best defense was a strong offense. At 1:30 P.M., the consortium took action after pooling their funds. Morgan floor broker Richard Whitney strode onto the NYSE floor, stopped at Post Number Two, and purchased 10,000 shares of U.S. Steel—for $10 more per share than the last buyer had paid. Whitney, a longtime board member of the New York Stock Exchange, was serving as acting president of the Exchange at the time. He was also a prominent floor broker for Morgan and Company. His credentials did as much to inspire confidence as did his act of bravado. Whitney and the bankers' consortium managed to curb runaway sell-ing for the rest of the day. A few stocks even gained ground as people followed Whitney's lead and began to purchase shares.

The large New York investment bank J. P. Morgan and Company, directed by Thomas Lamont (left) and J. P. Morgan Jr. (right), organized financial support for the NYSE that temporarily halted falling stock prices.

The market's "recovery" was deceptive, however. The more active stocks that made up the Dow-Jones average may have gotten a boost from the bankers' organized support, but less popular stocks continued to plummet in price. Moreover, many people were already ruined by the time the bankers stepped in to save the stock market. By the time trading closed for the day, the ticker lagged four hours behind actual trading. This meant that many of those who had sold early in order to minimize the damage to their fortunes ended up even worse off than they could have imagined.

On Friday, October 25, activity on the NYSE trading floor commenced in an orderly fashion. The volume of trading was still heavy at about 6 million shares. But something slightly sinister was taking place, unbeknownst to most investors. The bankers who had so gallantly stepped in just one day earlier to bull up the ailing market were now starting to quietly sell off the shares they had purchased to end Black Thursday. They sold the stock gradually to avoid triggering a panic. It was especially crucial that they not draw attention to this activity: 35 brokerage houses had placed ads in that day's papers urging people to buy stocks at once while prices were low!

Saturday, October 26, saw the New York Stock Exchange opened for a special short session—much to the chagrin of many overwhelmed brokers who were still trying to catch up after the previous week's mayhem. A few big investors tried to instill confidence and trigger more stock purchases by buying blocks of stock, but prices continued to slide down. Wall Street brokers worked on Sunday, too, still receiving and processing sell orders. As the brokers toiled, Congress pondered regulations to control speculation. But even if such measures had come to pass, they would have proved too little, too late.

On Monday, October 28, people looked to the New York bankers to provide a second massive dose of organized support, but they gave no more. The bankers did, however, eliminate air pockets on the market by buying stocks that could not otherwise be sold. Most margin accounts had already been sold out from under their holders; even those who had bought their shares with cash were selling out in droves. There was no late afternoon price rally on the Exchange floor. Although prices appeared to stabilize somewhat during the early afternoon, this was a passing phenomenon that amounted to nothing.

At 4:30 P.M. on October 28, the bankers' consortium made it official: they would not orchestrate any more support efforts. This announcement induced a sinking feeling in all but the most optimistic investors.

Taking their cue from the bankers' announcement, shareholders traded nearly 16.5 million stocks on October 29. Market conditions deteriorated so much that this date earned the nickname "Black Tuesday." The 40-member New York Stock Exchange Board of Governors met to discuss the merits of closing down the exchange. The board was undecided, fearing that a shutdown might trigger an unprecedented money panic. Unable to reach a decision, board members met again that evening, eventually agreeing that the exchange should remain open. In the hours between the board's first and second meetings, the market had stabilized enough to convince the board to postpone shutting down the New York Stock Exchange.

Even as journalists and economists were proclaiming the end of good times on the stock market, New York City banks continued dispensing brokers' loans. The city's banks had become many stockbrokers' only source of cash for financing speculation. Out-of-town banks and large corporations that had loaned money in better times had since recalled billions of dollars, leaving

STAGE   BROADWAY   SCREEN

VARIETY

PRICE 25¢.

VOL. XCVII. No. 3   NEW YORK, WEDNESDAY, OCTOBER 30, 1929   88 PAGES

WALL ST. LAYS AN EGG

Going Dumb Is Deadly to Hostess In Her Serious Dance Hall Profesh

DROP IN STOCKS ROPES SHOWMEN

Kidding Kissers in Talkers Burns Up Fans of Screen's Best Lovers

The banner headline of the October 29 edition of the show-business newspaper *Variety* says it all.

many brokerage houses in dire straits. New York City bankers met twice on October 29. The city banks wanted to fill the void left by those institutions that had recalled their money. They reduced the percentage of cash they required brokers to put down on bank loans from 40 percent to 25 percent. Brokerage firms limited available margin to no more than 25 percent (it had been as low as 10 percent earlier in 1929) to discourage risky speculation without bringing trading to a standstill.

On October 31, the Federal Reserve Board reduced the rediscount rate from 6 percent to 5 percent to discourage bank runs. It also started buying bonds to deter people from rushing to banks to withdraw cash.

From Friday, November 1 to Monday, November 4, the New York Stock Exchange closed for a long weekend. This was no holiday for brokerage firms or the support personnel who worked on the Exchange floor, however. They worked to correct clerical errors made during the previous week's fatiguing crush of sell orders. They also continued to execute sell orders, even though trading was suspended.

When the Exchange reopened for business on November 4, some diehard speculators were actually lured back into the game by the astonishingly low stock prices. A few even took out new margin accounts in order to grab up as many shares as their credit would allow. Some big companies tried to coax their sagging stock prices back to health by investing in large blocks of their own shares. But nothing worked. The Stock Market Crash of 1929 was not a single catastrophic event, but a series of financial calamities that culminated on October 29—Black Tuesday. Despair gathered over Wall Street like a storm cloud that stubbornly refused to discharge its rain and lighting.

By Halloween of 1929, the Stock Market Crash had become an inescapable fact. Although many people mark Black Tuesday as the "official" start of the Crash and the subsequent Great Depression, it is perhaps more truthful to state that a dramatic, seemingly bottomless slump began in the stock market on that day and soon infected all sectors of the American economy. The Dow-Jones average—once cause for optimism that bordered on hysteria when it peaked at 381—would continue to tumble, with only short reprieves along the way until it reached a low of 41 on July 8, 1933.

The country was already sliding into the Great Depression by November 13, 1929, when the closing Dow-Jones average of 224 led many people to wonder just how bad things could get. They didn't have long to wonder. The Great Depression toppled many of the upper class from their accustomed places in society, and blurred the line between a middle-class existence and a life of poverty for many others. The years between 1929 and the nation's entry into World War II in 1941 would test the mettle of Americans in ways that even the most farsighted among them probably never imagined.

Farm Foreclosures and Food Lines

6

The term "Great Depression" evokes black-and-white images of thin men in threadbare suits and worn-out shoes selling five-cent apples on city streets, of grim-faced women lined up three deep to collect bread and milk at relief stations. While pictures such as these may be indelibly etched into the consciousness of anyone who has studied 20th-century history, we frequently overlook another segment of American life: farmers. They may have been able to subsist on their own produce or crops during these desperate years, but few farmers could break even when they took their wares to market.

The farm economy had been in a state of crisis since the mid-1920s. American farmers had enjoyed a brief period of prosperity in the wake of World War I when the United States helped feed people in Europe until native farmers could recover from the disruption and devastation of war, but when this extra demand for farm products dried up, prices sagged. Wall Street's troubles further weakened the farmer's tenuous hold on financial survival. By 1932, farm prices would fall so low that the occupation of farming would actually cost more money than it yielded. Farmers frequently burned crops as fuel for heating and cooking, since doing so had become far cheaper than using coal.

An Iowa farmer named Milo Reno tried to counteract rock bottom farm prices by forming a union of sorts called the Farm Holiday Association. He encouraged other farmers to become activists. Those who joined the Farm Holiday movement destroyed their animals and crops—and those of nonparticipating farmers when the opportunity presented itself. They would set up blockades to intercept other farmers on their way to market and forcibly dump their milk, eggs, and produce.

Why would farmers waste their own cash crops—or destroy those of others? Reno and the Farm Holiday Association wanted to create a scarcity of farm products by destroying many of them before they reached the market. When demand finally outstripped supply, they reasoned, farm prices would climb again.

Even if they did not embrace the Farm Holiday Movement, whole communities sometimes resorted to extreme behavior in order to preserve family farms. Because it was so hard for farmers to make a living during the Depression years, many were unable to repay the banks that had loaned them the money to buy their farms. It was common for the banks to foreclose on the mortgages by taking away the property. Some judges and sheriffs who tried to carry out foreclosures on farm mortgages found themselves in real physical danger. Angry farmers and their neighbors routinely threatened them. When those threats became reality, the results ranged from beatings to episodes of public tarring and feathering.

Some farming communities used subtler means to protest foreclosures. When a foreclosed farm came up for auction at a sheriff's sale, the bidding would often be curiously low. This was because the farmer's friends and neighbors would agree before-hand to offer only pennies for each plow, horse, or parcel of land on the auction block. After purchasing every item at ridiculously low prices, the foreclosed farmer's friends returned everything to him or her.

In the midwestern and southern plains, the situation went from bad to worse. From 1931 to 1939, nature amplified the manmade disaster of the Depression as drought began to render entire farms lifeless. Years of light rainfall, accompanied by heavy plowing and grazing, had robbed the topsoil of its protective sod layer. With no sod to keep it in place, the topsoil sailed through the air, darkening the skies and filling the

Drought in the Midwest forced thousands of family farmers to leave their land in search of work. Some families moved to large cities like New York, Philadelphia, or Chicago; others, such as this mother and her children, went to California and subsisted as migrant laborers in fruit orchards.

lungs of whoever ventured outdoors. Dust storms deposited thick grime in doorways and windows. The dirt adhered to laundry on clotheslines and to anything else left outdoors.

The desperation engendered by the "Dustbowl" crept into other parts of the country when "Arkies" and "Okies" (derogatory nicknames for people from Arkansas and Oklahoma) migrated to other parts of the country in search of farm work. Many found their way to California's fertile San Joaquin Valley, only to discover that there wasn't much work to go around. As a result, these semi-nomadic laborers were easy targets for exploitation by farm owners, who routinely underpaid them. Many teetered on the brink of starvation as they went from place to place with the few possessions they still owned.

As some rural Americans destroyed "surplus" milk, grains, and meat, others had no prospect of feeding themselves. Like farming, the mining industry was already on shaky ground well before 1929. When the Depression's devitalizing fingers reached into Appalachia, coal mines reduced their hours or closed altogether. A West Virginia miner named Aaron Barkham estimated that as many as four out of five miners were unemployed in his community.

The Great Depression definitely increased the miserable living conditions of the miners, but part of their suffering was directly attributable to the business practices of mining companies. Even when mines did not close during the Depression, companies frequently swept aside men who had reached their late thirties or early forties and hired younger workers. Mining companies typically built and owned the towns around the mines. They charged their employees rent to live in the houses (or shacks). They also ran the stores, where they set high prices for food, toiletries, and other staples. This left out-of-work miners with no alternative sources of food or shelter when they could no longer pay the company's rates.

During the Great Depression, rural Americans longed to escape the grim conditions on the farms and in the mines. Some actually did pack up and move to large cities, believing that their prospects for gainful employment would improve. Unfortunately, these new urban dwellers were usually wrong.

Cities were already unable to support their native populations during the Depression; the influx of new residents made competition for jobs even keener. According to the Franklin Delano Roosevelt National Library, unemployment peaked at 24.9 percent of the country's total work force—12,830,000 people—in 1933. Among workers who kept their jobs, wages fell 42.5 percent from 1929 to 1933. Consumer demand for all kinds of goods and services decreased because people had little money to spend. This decreased demand forced employers to eliminate still more jobs. Since people visited doctors less frequently, even new medical school graduates often had difficulty finding work. Because people had little money to put away—and because so many people panicked and withdrew their money from banks—nearly 1,000 U. S. banks failed in 1931–32 alone.

Many people who had previously disdained any form of charity for the poor now reluctantly added their own names to state and local relief lists. Resourceful urban souls did whatever they could think

For urban residents in the 1930s, long lines became common: unemployment lines (top) and soup lines (at right).

of to survive without, or supplement, charitable financial assistance. Some sold surplus apples for a nickel apiece; others hawked handmade clothing or became shoeshine vendors. Despite people's sometimes heroic efforts to stay off relief, city charities found themselves strapped for funds by the early 1930s.

There was not enough relief to aid everyone who needed it. In the winter of 1932 alone, New York City hospitals reported 95 cases of starvation with 20 confirmed deaths. Many of those who survived were malnourished from subsisting on cheap foods like candy, Chinese noodles, and biscuits for days at a time. People also "stretched" complete meals when they

could afford them by doing things like doubling a batch of gravy with extra water and flour. It is ironic to note that while many Americans found it extremely difficult to feed themselves and their families, food prices were at a low point. Bread may have cost less than a dime a loaf, but few people could afford to shop as they had before the Depression.

"Food lines" became common sights on city streets. The fare varied from day to day. Sometimes people lined up to receive a sandwich and coffee; other times, children waited to collect pails of donated soup for themselves and their families. Accepting food line handouts was difficult for people who had prided themselves on providing for themselves.

Just as rural farmers banded together to resist foreclosures, many city dwellers came to feel bound together by their hardships. They shared what they had with friends and neighbors. In some cases, the Great Depression broke down social barriers and equalized relationships between people who were formerly of different socioeconomic classes. One black man who was growing up in Chicago at this time wryly noted that his father's restaurant seemed to have a favorable impact on neighborhood race relations:

> My family always had a lot of white friends because there was always some food. A white friend would forget his supposedly superior attitude if there's food involved. They were going to get some of my father's mystical fried chicken.

Although some Americans responded to the Depression with a new sense of unity and concern for others, the experience was hardly a tonic for the nation's societal ills. Many of the rich suffered a stunning blow to their fortunes, but the poor grew destitute. As competition for work tightened in both rural and urban areas, blacks—who were discriminated against even in good economic times—found that their difficulties in the job market increased dramatically. Author Milton Meltzer says that as many as 56 percent of African-American workers were unemployed in 1932.

People who had only a few years earlier anticipated a future of abundant wealth discovered that the proverbial rug had been pulled out from under them during the 1930s. Fortunes were lost in the Crash before children and grandchildren could inherit them.

Some distraught heads of household saw only one dark alternative to watching their families struggle—they committed suicide so that their survivors could collect cash on life insurance policies.

As their prospects ran out, those hardest hit by the Depression formed shantytowns called "Hoovervilles" on the outskirts of cities and towns. These makeshift encampments made from old crates, auto bodies, and other found objects were scathingly named for the incumbent president. Herbert Hoover's seeming indifference to the Depression angered people so much that they began naming any evidence of their poverty after him. When a family out West sat down to a supper of

The shacks and shanties of the unemployed were nicknamed "Hoovervilles," a sarcastic reference to the president under whose watch the Depression had begun.

sinewy jackrabbit for lack of anything else to eat, they might speak of dining on "Hoover Hog."

Some nomadic souls became hoboes, riding the rails on "Hoover Pullmans," or freight cars. One estimate places the number of people who at least tried the hobo life during the 1930s at 250,000. People took to the trains for any number of reasons during the Depression. Some rode around the country searching for work. Some wandered out of aimlessness, hopelessness, or simple boredom. Hoboes frequently formed loose affiliations with each other to consolidate whatever food they could scrounge, beg, shoplift, or buy. They also occasionally tipped each other off about job prospects in a given area.

Some people weathered the Depression with a "We're all in this together" mentality that fostered a spirit of sharing and kindness. But others felt unrelenting desperation that led them to violence. The country experienced isolated instances of rioting due to food shortages, violent handling of labor disputes, and other bloody episodes related to the Depression. One labor uprising occurred in 1932 in Dearborn, Michigan, when unemployed laborers marched on Ford's River Rouge automotive plant. Police fired on them, killing four and wounding fifty. On Memorial Day in 1937, steelworkers on Chicago's south side were picketing Republic Steel when tear gas and gunfire were unleashed upon them, killing 10 and wounding many more.

During the Depression, workers had little recourse against layoffs, reduced hours, job discrimination, and low pay. Unions were formed to protect workers from unfair practices. For every worker who was unwilling to work under harsh conditions, however, many more

would gladly take his or her place. Exploitation became common as workers grew increasingly desperate for jobs after long stretches of unemployment.

One of the most shocking instances of violence that occurred during the Great Depression was prompted by the arrival of the Bonus Army in Washington, D.C. The Bonus Army was a group made up of thousands of World War I army veterans whose need for money spurred them to become activists. To reward the army veterans for their valor in World War I, Congress had passed a law in 1924 that granted them federal insurance policies. The law stipulated that the veterans had

In 1932 the Bonus Army marched to Washington to urge Congress to allow World War I veterans to cash in government-granted insurance policies. When Congress refused, some 4,000 veterans refused to leave the capital, camping out on the outskirts of Washington, D.C.

to hold these policies until 1945, after which they could collect cash on them. By the spring of 1932, however, many of the veterans were in dire financial straits. They wanted to cash in on their policies immediately.

Out of this desperation, the Bonus Army was born. World War I veterans and their family members came to the Washington, D.C., area by train, by car, and on foot. That summer, some 20,000 people were camped out around the White House, intent on lobbying Congress to let them collect on their insurance policies. Most of them stayed on Anacostia Flats along the Potomac River.

Congress introduced a bill to the Senate on the issue. When the Senate defeated the measure, 4,000 outraged members of the Bonus Army refused to disband and go home. By July 28, the Hoover Administration had had enough.

President Hoover ordered the 12th Infantry—led by Army chief of staff Douglas MacArthur and assisted by officers George S. Patton and Dwight Eisenhower—to drive the Bonus Army out of Washington. As the U.S. Army closed in on the Bonus Army's encampments, some of the veterans initially thought that their younger counterparts were coming to show their support.

They could not have been more incorrect. The 12th Infantry fired upon the veterans. Bonus Army camps were set afire, and their occupants were chased across the Potomac River and out of the capital. Injuries ranged from gunshot wounds and cuts to ears sheared off by Army sabers. When the skirmish was over, four marchers were dead. President Hoover offered to pay for the veterans' trip home.

The veterans were eventually permitted to redeem their insurance policies for cash in the spring of 1936, rather than waiting another nine years. For those who witnessed it, the attack on the Bonus Army was an unforgettabe episode in American history. One witness later likened the scene to "sons attacking their fathers."

During the Great Depression, many Americans discovered a new capacity for thrift, ingenuity, and kindness in themselves and others. The effects of the nation's collapsed economy also had a pronounced dark side, however. Hunger, hardship, and fear of what the future held drove some to give up, grow embittered, or become violent. The dynamic, optimistic nation that had reveled through the Roaring Twenties seemed to be in a state of suspended animation. People waited for something—anything—to indicate a reversal of their declining fortunes.

Without money, people found it nearly impossible to provide for their basic needs or to hold on to their dreams. Many lost houses in which they had grown up. Countless students had to abandon their hopes for a college education. In many cases, even a high school diploma was an unattainable luxury because young people needed to work to help support their families.

As surely as the Great Depression dried up people's cash supplies and employment opportunities, it also depleted their hope. The nation would soon elect a new president who would replenish this intangible resource by changing the way the government worked.

During his first 100 days
in office, President
Franklin Delano Roosevelt
introduced a flurry of legislation intended to end
the Great Depression.

One Hundred Days

In the days after the Crash, President Hoover appeared reluctant to publicly reassure people that things would quickly improve, despite mounting pressure to do so. And the treatment of the Bonus Army did nothing to help Herbert Hoover's public image. The incident made him appear increasingly callous to the travails of ordinary Americans and oblivious to their desperation.

In truth, Hoover was a complicated individual who happened to be president of the United States at a very inopportune time. That he could have done anything to prevent the crash of 1929 is hardly a foregone conclusion—especially since he took office a mere seven months before the stock market collapsed. But many considered President

Hoover unfeeling for his minimal and indirect response to the Great Depression.

In 1932, the Hoover Administration did make an attempt to infuse new life into the economy with federal money. It created the Reconstruction Finance Corporation (RFC), a government entity to provide financial assistance. But the RFC awarded some $2 billion chiefly to banks and big businesses, leaving only a tiny amount for state relief funds. The president hoped to restart the economic engines of big business and banking by infusing them with a fresh supply of cash. The resulting surge of commercial activity would in turn send money "trickling down" to workers. Unfortunately, very little trickling went on, and the RFC ultimately had little impact on daily life for most people.

Even if Hoover's program had worked as planned, the RFC would probably still have been widely regarded as too little, too late. On November 8, 1932, Franklin Delano Roosevelt (FDR) defeated Herbert Hoover in the presidential election. The two-term governor of New York had chosen Speaker of the House John Nance Garner as his vice president.

Although Roosevelt was no newcomer to politics, he had overcome tremendous personal obstacles to assume the presidency. He had been stricken with poliomyelitis (polio, infantile paralysis) during the summer of 1921. This viral infection killed or crippled numerous Americans—mostly children—until Jonas Salk developed the first successful vaccine in 1954. Roosevelt's bout with polio left him paralyzed from the waist down. He would never regain the use of his legs.

But FDR was determined to reclaim his power and vigor to the fullest possible extent. He went to Florida

and practiced a grueling, self-imposed swimming reg-
imen until he could propel himself through the water
with seeming ease. In addition to resuming his career
in law and public service, FDR became a tireless crusader against polio, taking a special interest in children
affected by the disease. He funded the Georgia Warm
Springs Foundation—a treatment facility in Warm
Springs, Georgia, where recovering polio patients
could bathe in warm springs in the hope of regaining
the use of their paralyzed muscles. In 1938 FDR
founded the National Foundation for Infantile Paralysis; this organization later became the March of Dimes,
which today strives to prevent and cure a variety of dis-
abling conditions.

After his election to the presidency, FDR defied the
odds once more. He survived an assassination attempt
while making a public appearance in Miami, Florida. A
man named Guiseppe Zangara fired on Roosevelt and
his companions. Zangara's gunshot missed FDR, but it
mortally wounded Chicago mayor Anthony Cermak.

Fortunately, the remaining days before Roosevelt's
inauguration proved less eventful. He took the oath of
office at 1:08 P.M. on March 4, 1933. It was a cloudy,
raw, and drizzly Saturday, but a crowd gathered at the
east front of the Capitol building to hear their new
leader's inaugural address. President Roosevelt's words
rang confidently against a backdrop of dreary weather
and daunting economic conditions.

"Only a foolish optimist can deny the dark realities
of the moment," he told his audience. Roosevelt's
speech had a moral urgency about it as he alluded to
stock market speculation, singling it out as a cause of
the country's current plight:

The money changers have fled from their high seats in the temple of our civilization. We may now restore that temple to the ancient truths. The measure of the restoration lies in the extent to which we apply social values more noble than mere monetary profit.

Happiness lies not in the mere possession of money; it lies in the joy of achievement, in the thrill of creative effort. The joy and moral stimulation of work no longer must be forgotten in the mad chase of evanescent profits. These dark days will be worth all they cost us if they teach us that our true destiny is not to be ministered unto but to minister to ourselves and to our fellow men.

The new president wasted no time. The entire package of reforms he introduced from his inauguration until the start of World War II came to be known as the New Deal. But the period from March 5 to June 16, 1933, was characterized by so much legislative activity that it had a name all its own: the Hundred Days. In just over three months, the Roosevelt Administration passed 15 major laws and numerous smaller bills.

On Monday, March 6, FDR initiated a four-day national "Bank Holiday." The holiday proclamation also included a provision forbidding people from exporting gold or redeeming currency for gold. The new president took America off the gold standard in order to replenish the depleted supply of gold in America's banking system. Although bankers across the country feared that this would dramatically weaken banks, or that the impending four-day shutdown would trigger devastating bank runs, neither crisis occurred. The president planned to stagger the bank reopenings, with the soundest banks resuming business on Friday, March 10. Some banks were so depleted by the Crash that they would never operate again, however.

While the banks were closed, some merchants made their own scrip (paper currency or tokens for use in emergencies) so that people could shop in local stores even if they were temporarily out of cash. Some customers bought food on credit or good faith at their neighborhood groceries. Being caught without cash on hand seemed to be a great equalizer of people. One man who worked as a margin clerk at a brokerage firm when the Crash occurred shared his recollections of the Bank Holiday with Studs Terkel in *Hard Times:*

> The Bank Holiday of 1933 brought a certain kind of joyous, devil-may-care mood. People were just gettin' along somehow. It was based on the theory: Good grief, it couldn't get much worse. They bartered things for things.

On the following Sunday, March 12, FDR delivered a radio broadcast to discuss the previous week's Bank Holiday in a relaxed, informal fashion. He thanked the American people for putting up with the temporary hardships that resulted from the shutdown. The president then explained that during the past week, the Bureau of Engraving and Printing had been issuing "sound currency" to replenish banks across the country. Regular national radio broadcasts soon became a Roosevelt staple. In these "fireside chats," FDR offered reassurance and explanations as he implemented reforms at a rapid pace. As confidence in the banking system returned, stock prices temporarily experienced a modest increase.

Roosevelt's next move was to ensure the passage of

The Civilian Conservation Corps provided work for young unemployed men. Housed in old Army camps, the CCC members improved and maintained national parks, planted trees, built and repaired dams, and participated in other improvement projects.

the Twenty-First Amendment, which ended Prohibition by nullifying the Eighteenth Amendment. The president recognized that the social experiment of Prohibition had failed to create a "dry" nation and instead had spawned a thriving underworld industry. He reasoned that the legal manufacture and sale of alcoholic beverages would boost the economy, so he brought liquor back from the shady speakeasies of the 1920s and into the world of legitimate business.

But while the repeal of Prohibition meant that breweries and distilleries could reopen, a single enterprise could only employ so many people. "Our greatest primary task is to put people to work," Roosevelt had said in his inaugural address:

> This is no unsolvable problem if we face it wisely and courageously. It can be accomplished in part by direct recruiting by the Government itself, treating the task as we would treat the emergency of a war, but at the same time, through this employment, accomplishing greatly needed projects to stimulate and reorganize the use of our natural resources.

The President's solution was the creation of the Civilian Conservation Corps (CCC), or "Three Cs." The CCC accepted young, unmarried men who preferred productive employment to public relief. They lived on old Army camps throughout the country. Under the supervision of army personnel, the Civilian Conservation Corps improved and maintained national parks, planted trees, built and repaired dams, and performed other projects. The Corps members received free room and board, plus a monthly stipend of $30.

One former member named Blackie Gold told

author Studs Terkel that he "really enjoyed" his three separate CCC assignments—planting trees, fighting forest fires, and planting still more trees. "I had three wonderful square meals a day," he said, crediting Civilian Conservation Corps with making him into a man.

The degree of warmth with which the Corps was received varied as much as the towns in which the men stayed. When they left their bases and visited the surrounding communities, some CCC members met their future wives while others were harassed. Regardless of how locals felt about the CCC men, however, their presence was financially beneficial. That was because FDR budgeted $500 million in relief money for distribution among states that sponsored CCC programs.

By the time the start of World War II eliminated the need for the CCC, some 2.5 million young men had passed through the program. The Civilian Conservation Corps had given them the opportunity to earn money and to help support family members back home, where jobs were scarce. The CCC's accomplishments went beyond getting able-bodied men off of public relief, though. In the drought-stricken Plains region, for example, the Corps planted millions of trees. This helped to correct the soil conditions that had led to the problems of the Dust Bowl.

The so-called alphabet agencies of the Roosevelt administration also helped America's farmers. The Agricultural Adjustment Act (AAA) paid farmers to cut back on production. Farmers who agreed to reduce their acreage for growing wheat and corn during 1933 qualified for benefits. Those who raised cotton destroyed a percentage of their crops, since it was too late in the growing season to cut back on acreage. Hog farmers agreed to slaughter a certain number of extra pigs in order to collect aid. Although nobody got terribly worked up about the destruction of crops, the slaughter of about six million pigs and piglets provoked public outcries against waste and cruelty. At first, the government did waste some of this surplus meat, but it soon went to feed the needy.

Even with measures in place to cut farm production, however, some surplus was still inevitable. The AAA permitted the president to sell any extra farm products on the international market for whatever prices they would fetch. Farm prices rose in response to FDR's double-pronged approach of less production and more selling. Despite its success, however, the AAA was ruled unconstitutional in 1936 on the grounds that the government was interfering with free trade. Congress reworked the bill, however, and the new AAA became law in 1938.

The Farm Credit Association (FCA) was an agency that saved farms from foreclosure by purchasing outstanding mortgages from private companies. The FCA would then take over the mortgages and lower the interest payments to farmers so that they could hold on to their homes, land, and equipment.

In April 1933, the Tennessee Valley Authority (TVA) was born. This agency went to work on May 18, rehabilitating an idle power plant that stood along the Tennessee River in Muscle Shoals, Alabama. The government had built the hydroelectric plant during World War I at a cost of $165 million—and then never activated it. When the TVA started up the plant, it supplied farmers throughout the Tennessee Valley with affordable electricity. A regiment of the CCC did conservation work on the land surrounding the plant to prevent flooding and erosion.

Roosevelt's Hundred Days legislation also brought reform to America's cities and towns. The National Industrial Recovery Act (NIRA) was designed to increase employment. To lower costs during the Depression, many financially strapped employers had drastically pared down their work forces, then given the remaining employees many more hours at low wages. The NIRA established a limit on the number of hours per week one employee could work, in order to distribute jobs more evenly, and also established a minimum wage to help those who had jobs earn enough to support themselves and their families without federal aid.

Secretary of Labor Frances Perkins was one of the masterminds of both the CCC and the NIRA. Perkins, a former social worker, was the first woman ever to serve in the Cabinet, a collection of top advisors to the president. She had known FDR since her days as a lobbyist in New York when he was that state's governor. President Roosevelt was so impressed by her intelligence and energy that when he reached the White House, he asked Perkins to be his secretary of labor.

During the final stages of the Hundred Days, Congress introduced two more pieces of legislation to increase the American people's sense of security. The establishment of the Home Owners' Loan Corporation (HOLC) was proposed on June 13. It was designed to help homeowners in the same way that the Farm Credit Association aided farmers faced with foreclosure. The HOLC took over and refinanced home mortgages of people who had defaulted on their payments. As people took advantage of the opportunity to make a fresh start with mortgage payments they could handle, the number of new home starts and home sales increased nationwide.

The Banking Act of 1933 was the last law enacted during the Hundred Days. The act provided for the creation of the Federal Depositors' Insurance Corporation (FDIC), a federal entity that guaranteed people access to their money. Deposits of up to $10,000 made to member banks were guaranteed against losses like those incurred during the bank runs of the Stock Market Crash. (Deposits are insured up to $100,000 today.) The Banking Act was very effective in preventing bank failures. In fact, since the inception of the FDIC, the total number of annual bank failures across the country has consistently numbered in the single digits. (By contrast, there were nearly 1,000 bank failures nationwide in 1931–32.)

The Hundred Days ended on June 16, 1933, when Congress adjourned for a much-needed break. Although this date marked the end of the most intensive spurt of legislative activity in FDR's presidency, the New Deal was hardly complete. Among the programs introduced after the Hundred Days was the Securities and Exchange Commission (SEC). The SEC was founded in 1934 to watch over the formerly "self-regulating" stock market.

The Works Progress Administration (WPA) began creating jobs for everyone from unemployed welders and teachers to actors and musicians in 1935. One offshoot of the WPA was the National Youth Administration (NYA), a program that offered high school and college students part-time jobs, allowing them to stay in school during the Depression.

A merchant puts up a National Recovery Administration poster, featuring the NRA's blue eagle, in his store window.

By 1934, the Hundred Days was starting to yield some measurable results. Americans were working in some 5 million new jobs, boosting the entire economy as they became better able to afford some of the goods and services they had enjoyed before the Depression.

The Hundred Days was not a complete, unconditional success, however. The National Recovery Administration (NRA) was spearheaded by a colorful character named Hugh "Ironpants" Johnson. He wanted to promote business growth and prevent price slumps by eliminating product surpluses. Johnson got his unusual nickname because he was a former cavalryman—and because his stubbornness was legendary. He had a reputation for excessive crankiness, heavy drinking, and rough language. But the same people who found him difficult to work with also admired his intelligence and the breadth of his interests. Before joining FDR as the NRA administrator, for example, Johnson had written several acclaimed books for young readers.

But Johnson's intelligence could not guarantee the NRA's success. The administration attempted to regulate big businesses by encouraging them to form associations with the government. These business associations would then establish standards for the number of employees each member company could employ, how much product they could turn out, and at what prices they could sell their wares. The government tried to generate enthusiasm about the NRA by using a big blue eagle logo that appeared on the doors of participating businesses—and even on some items of clothing. Underneath the eagle was the slogan, "We do our part."

The sight of the blue eagle and the excitement that Johnson tried to generate surrounding its use led people to feel that at least something was being done to help revive American business. Employment and stock prices rose briefly in late 1933 in response to the implementation of the NRA. But this piece of New Deal legislation was fraught with problems.

Hugh Johnson's plan was too idealistic because it depended entirely on the good faith of competing businesses. Compliance with the NRA was not mandatory. That fact left plenty of nonparticipating manufacturers free to hire thinner work crews, produce more goods, and sell them at lower prices than companies that followed NRA quotas. Those who joined NRA-sanctioned associations were hardly cooperating harmoniously with other member companies, either. The biggest businesses in any given association routinely voted to institute rules that would work to their singular advantage.

In 1935, the NRA was declared unconstitutional. The organization violated fair trade laws because it encouraged the formation of trusts, or large conglomerate businesses that made it impossible for smaller, nonmember companies to compete with them.

In 1936, Franklin Delano Roosevelt defeated Republican opponent Alf Landon to win a second term in office. Although FDR had accomplished a great deal up to that point, the Depression persisted, and New Deal fever was slowly dying down. Several politicians arrived on the national scene during the mid-1930s, each attempting to steal FDR's thunder with a pioneering economic agenda designed to end the Depression once and for all. One of these was Louisiana senator Huey "Kingfish" Long, who gained a national following with his Share-Our-Wealth movement.

Share-Our-Wealth actually required only the rich to do any sharing. Long promised every American family a free house, car, and radio, plus an annual income of $2,000 (just about enough to raise a family of four at the time). He called for the redistribution of America's money by imposing an $8 million cap on the amount of money any one person could accumulate through earnings. Anyone who inherited wealth would be permitted to keep a maximum of $5 million under Long's plan. The government would confiscate the rest to finance his vision for middle-class America.

As preposterous as Senator Long's proposal sounds

to us today, he had actually generated enough interest during the Depression to consider entering the 1936 presidential race. He never faced FDR or Alf Landon on the campaign trail, though. Long's assassination on September 8, 1935, in Baton Rouge, Louisiana, put an end to any serious development of the Share-Our-Wealth movement.

The Roosevelt administration had no intention of taking from the rich to give to the poor. But FDR and his cabinet did recognize that Share-Our-Wealth had been attractive to so many people because they saw no other way of providing for themselves and their families. For all the jobs the New Deal had created, unemployment remained high. Some people had seen their working years come to an end during the Depression years. Now that they had reached retirement age, their job prospects were practically nonexistent, and unemployment had depleted any "nest egg" they may have saved for their later years.

In response to the needs of these older Americans, Congress passed the Social Security Act in 1935. It mostly concerned payments to senior citizens, and the government paid out its first benefits to the aged on January 31, 1940. But the Social Security Act also contained provisions for disabled people and a measure for Aid to Dependent Children (ADC). The original intent of ADC was to provide benefits to the survivors of miners, who were particularly hard-hit during the Depression. Today, ADC payments serve children from low-income families in a variety of situations while Social Security payments continue to supplement the income of retired Americans.

When President Roosevelt defeated Wendell

President Franklin Delano Roosevelt signs the Social Security Act into law in 1935. Behind FDR to the right is Secretary of Labor Frances Perkins, the first female member of a presidential cabinet and an important contributor to many of Roosevelt's New Deal programs.

Wilkie in the 1940 election, he was not without his detractors. The New Deal had brought about lasting changes in the way the government responded to disadvantaged people. Even temporary measures like the CCC inspired later programs based on work in exchange for federal assistance. The creation of jobs during the depths of the Depression had brought renewed hope and purpose to millions of American lives. Despite the ambitious scope of the New Deal, however, the Depression did not go away. Some people consequently viewed FDR as a misguided crusader whose liberal spending of government money failed to pull America out of the economic abyss.

Of course, the Depression did finally end. The benchmark history uses to denote the economy's return to health is America's entry into World War II. President Roosevelt declared war on Japan, Italy, and Germany on December 8, 1941, following the bombing of Pearl Harbor. War created an immediate need for full employment—of men and women alike—in factories that manufactured tanks, planes, and other military vehicles and implements. In fact, some commercial factories were retooled to serve the defense industry. Because the need for workers was so great, the government prohibited labor strikes. American farmers found that their business improved, too. For the first time in years, they were scrambling to increase production in order to help feed the American and Allied troops (Britain, France, the USSR, and Canada).

American entry into World War II lifted the Great Depression, but at a great cost to the friends and families of those who served. Some 10 to 12 million workers were unemployed during the Depression years; during World War II, that figure dropped to fewer than 1 million. War proved to be a surefire—albeit bloody—way of ending the Great Depression. But could a stock market collapse recur in the future?

Americans had a brush with this hypothetical terror in 1987.

DAILY◉NEWS

NEW YORK'S PICTURE NEWSPAPER®

5¢   Tuesday, October 20, 19

PANIC!

Dow plunges through floor — 508 pts

6 PAGES OF COMPLETE COVERAGE BEGIN ON PAGE 2

Could It Happen Again?

With the advent of World War II, the Great Depression came to an end, although America faced a new set of trials. The Depression had been a worldwide crisis that threatened the very future of capitalism. America inadvertently contributed to the collapse of the world economy by decreasing the amount of money it pumped into foreign loans and imports. In 1929, America's overseas investments totaled $200 million; in the 1930s, that figure averaged only $60 million a year. The United States also placed prohibitively expensive tariffs (taxes) on imported goods. In 1930, the Hawley-Smoot Tariff was passed, placing a 50 percent tax charge on imports. Hawley-Smoot was an attempt to protect American interests by encouraging people to buy products made in the United States. But it did more harm than good, touching off a tariff war in which other countries retaliated by setting high tariffs of their own.

With demand for imported goods down worldwide, the depression spread. In Germany, for instance, two-thirds of the labor force was either unemployed or employed only part-time. In some British towns, unemployment reached 80 percent. Numerous French workers lost their jobs after 1932, but at least as many farmers suffered in isolation as their livelihood slipped away. Unemployment sidelined approximately one-third of all workers in the Netherlands.

Different nations had different ways of coping with the adversity that enveloped them. In Germany, the depression gave Adolf Hitler a foothold. Heavy public spending was part of the Nazi government's agenda, and the infusion of public money helped lift that country out of its economic depression by the late 1930s. Other economically depressed nations did not recover until after the start of World War II.

The devastation that worked its way through the world economy during the 1930s made it impossible for stock markets to rebound. In America, the New York Stock Exchange—and other exchanges around the nation—had to struggle through the 1930s before eventually recovering.

In 1943, women went to work on the trading floor at the New York Stock Exchange for the first time. They didn't leave when World War II ended in 1945, but this advance was not enough to change the entire Wall Street establishment's imposingly stuffy, buttoned-down image. The securities business tried

to make itself more accessible to "average" investors after World War II. In the words of author Dana L. Thomas, brokerage firms "set dead aim at the little old lady from Dubuque." They set up investment clubs and dispensed free advice to their customers in an effort to demystify the market and encourage people to invest their money. In 1954, the NYSE began its own educational campaign called "Own Your Share of American Business" in order to attract more investors.

These programs seem to have worked. A bigger proportion of Americans became stockholders after the war than had invested during the 1920s bull market.

This July 1943 photo shows one of the major changes that occurred on the New York Stock Exchange after the Great Depression—women, such as the ones pictured at the left counter, were permitted to work on the NYSE for the first time.

These new investors had some important distinguishing features, however. They typically owned fewer shares than those in the 1920s had, and as a group, they were not as heavily margined.

The stock market spent the early postwar years regaining vitality. Then, in 1954, prices took off on a bull run. When the market started to decline, it got a boost from an unexpected place: outer space. In October 1957, the Soviet Union had launched Sputnik I, the world's first artificial satellite. Production and stocks in the electronics industry boomed in 1958 as America's space program scurried to catch up with—and surpass—the USSR's.

As the volume of trading increased, so did the volume of paperwork. In 1968, the NYSE experienced what it termed a "paperwork crisis," with member companies working 24 hours a day to keep abreast of trading. Something had to change.

Change came in the form of computers. The Exchange became increasingly automated throughout the 1970s. Computers could process numbers faster than brains could. They could also extrapolate the best stocks to buy using pure logic—a task that had long eluded human beings. Brokerage houses could soon preprogram stop-loss orders, triggering automatic sales of a stock the instant its price fell below a predetermined level. Computers eliminated the need to talk with one's broker before massive blocks of stock were dumped onto the market with a single keystroke.

Computers became so sophisticated that they could detect irregularities in trading practices that might indicate insider trading. Insider trading is the buying and selling of securities based on secret information not available to the rest of the public. In the 1980s, insider trading was illegal; during the 1920s, it had taken place regularly.

Computers also linked the New York Stock Exchange to other exchanges around the world, transforming it into an influential branch office of the global stock exchange. This meant that any ripple felt on the NYSE would affect exchanges around the world more quickly than ever.

American spending habits during the 1980s eerily echoed those of the high-living 1920s in more than a few respects. People were buying what they wanted on easy credit terms. The country was soaring on a wave of economic health and power that was at least in part illusory as America was in fact a debtor nation to Japan and other countries. Money for consumer goods seemed plentiful, however, so few people were concerned.

This climate of comfort and affluence helped fuel a bull run on the stock market that began in August of 1982. The Reagan administration contributed to the boom by cutting income taxes to people with the highest earnings, who in turn invested their "extra" money in common stocks. The Dow-Jones Industrial Average seemed headed for an unprecedented 3,000 points by 1987. People ignored the fact that stock prices were fast outstripping real economic growth.

As the Dow peaked at 2,722.42 points on August 25, 1987, margin was available to those who wanted to "stretch" their investment. The Federal Reserve now had the power to require minimum deposits on margin accounts. Borrowers had to put at least 50 percent down on all margin accounts in 1987, as opposed to the low of 10 percent in 1929.

Despite these safeguards, there were some jitters on the market by late summer of 1987. Magazine articles reflected this nervousness. "Stock Prices: Getting Scary," intoned *Fortune* in September. "Time to Get out of the Market?" asked *U.S. News & World Report*'s August 31 issue. That same issue offered its readers another short piece entitled "What to Do If the Market Collapses: A Lifeboat, Just in Case," which reminded readers that stop-loss orders were a viable alternative to going down with the stock market if it collapsed.

Alarming headlines aside, most pundits didn't forecast a 1929-style crash. Speculation was neither as rampant nor as heavily margined in 1987 as it had been in 1929. In "Time to Get out of the Market?" *U. S. News & World Report* called Robert Prechter "the presiding guru over this bull market" and quoted his prediction that the Dow might soar as high as 3,700 points by the end of 1988 before declining.

But the market's behavior on Friday, October 16, indicated that perhaps the bull run was not going to last as long as Prechter had predicted. The Dow-Jones Industrial Average dropped by 100 points that day, which was a record loss for a single session. It turned out that Friday's slip was just a prelude to Monday, October 19. This was a day of decline so dramatic that it earned that dreadful distinction of being one of the New York Stock Exchange's "Black" days.

On "Black Monday" 1987, the Dow-Jones Average fell 508.32 points, from 2,247.72 to a closing index of 1738.40. Some 604 million shares changed hands as the Dow lost more than 22 percent of its value. Pandemonium ensued on the NYSE floor—thanks in part to computers.

Like its predecessor the ticker tape machine, the NYSE's computers could not keep up with the staggering volume of trade that took place on Black Monday. Ironically, it was computers themselves that helped make the job of recording up-to-the-minute transactions so difficult in 1987. This was because falling stock prices set off a cascade of preprogrammed stop-loss orders, dumping millions of shares onto the market at eye-blink speed. As hordes of panicked investors all ran for the same computerized escape hatch in the form of the preprogrammed stop-loss order, many companies made old-fashioned attempts to lure new buyers. They purchased huge blocks of their own stock, but failed to inspire much consumer confidence or interest.

The development of computers in the 1970s helped stockbrokers handle more and larger stock orders. However, the speed at which computers could process transactions could also create problems, as the 1987 crash illustrated.

Also, while a plunge in the stock markets of one country had long affected other foreign exchanges, computers now provided an instantaneous link between one nation's stock market debacle and the rest of the world. The impact of Black Monday was immediately felt on exchanges as far away as London and Tokyo. Japan was particularly hard-hit because its investors were heavily margined.

By Tuesday, October 20, 1987, the crash was ending—even though the volume of trade jumped to 608 million shares. In the aftermath of Black Monday, the computer's power and speed became its saving grace as making sense of the onslaught of sales was easier than it had been in 1929. Prices took nearly two years to regain all of their lost ground, but the economy kept chugging along during this recovery period.

The Federal Reserve Board, which by 1987 played a greater regulatory role in America's money supply, prevented Black Monday from leading to the kind of bottomless drop that characterized the Stock Market Crash of 1929. In 1987 the Fed controlled minimum margin requirements, enabling more investors to avoid being sold out in the event of a price slump—and protecting banks against bad brokers' loans. When the stock market collapsed on Black Monday, the Fed also promised to pump more cash into its banks if necessary, providing a measure of reassurance that was absent in 1929.

The nature of personal investing had also changed in ways that helped prevent the pervasive devastation of 1929. Then, investors as a rule told their brokers what to buy and kept close tabs on their stocks. In 1987, more private investors had diverse portfolios, managed by professionals who picked stocks for their customers, and who were less prone to fearful, knee-jerk selling in a crisis than were inexperienced market players.

This is not to say that there were no casualties on Black Monday. Thousands of investors were hurt. The crash prompted one known suicide and left behind plenty of case studies like the one that opened the November 23 cover story of *Business Weekly*:

> The investor, in his late 20s, had ridden the boom. Using risky, highly leveraged trading strategies, he had

built up his brokerage account . . . to a $700,000 balance. Now, two weeks after the crash, he sat in the office of [his broker], nearly in tears. His new balance: a margin debt that may reach $200,000.

Claims of "broker misconduct" soared after the 1987 stock market crash. Although brokerage clients typically received literature warning of the pitfalls of investing on margin, many claimed that their brokers failed to speak to them about these risks personally. Furthermore, disillusioned clients said they were frequently encouraged to take out margin accounts, because the brokers who opened them stood to earn extra commissions on margined customers. When the bottom dropped out of the market on Black Monday, many customers—margined or not—were alarmed to find that they could not get through to their brokers. In some cases, customers claimed that their brokerage firms actually hung up on them because they were unable to cope with the volume of incoming calls.

Despite the differences between the Great Crash of 1929 and Black Monday of 1987, the inevitable comparisons arose. Dana L. Thomas writes:

For millions of Americans born after 1929, who had never before experienced a serious panic on Wall Street, the realization sank in that the stock market was a two-way affair, and, as any market historian could have told them, it was as capable of going disastrously down as zestfully up.

Most economists say another stock market crash is probably in our future. As long as people are lured by the slim chance of getting rich quickly and with little

Stock market speculation will always be an uncertain science. This monitor in New York's Times Square is reporting on the Dow-Jones Industrial Average's largest-ever single-day point decline. On October 27, 1997, the Dow dropped 554.26 points, or 7.2 percent of its value, to close at 7,160.15.

effort, they will be drawn to the gamble that is stock market investing. It is a gamble that has paid off handsomely for many people in the past decade. Stock prices have grown at an incredible rate. It took the Dow-Jones Industrial Average from 1928 (when the index first included 30 stocks) to 1972 to reach 1,000. The Dow hit 2,000 for the first time 15 years later, in early 1987. After the 1987 crash, the market climbed back until the Dow surpassed 3,000 in April 1991. By February 1995, the Dow-Jones Industrial Average crossed the 4,000 level. In the next four years, the average would gain 6,000 more points, finally closing above 10,000 for the first time on March 29, 1999.

At the same time, more and more Americans are discovering the excitement of online investing— brokerless, low-fee Internet stock trading anytime, anywhere. As services like E-Trade skyrocket in popularity, it is possible Wall Street is courting a new generation of hair-trigger investors poised to jump out of the market as soon as the bull run ends.

America appears to be striding into the 21st century with a clean bill of economic health. Employment, home construction, and other indicators of the economy bespeak optimism, but the lessons of 1929 still linger. "While most economists say that a stock crash is unlikely any time soon," Charles Oliver wrote in the May 25, 1999, edition of *Investor's Business Daily*, "they've been keeping an eye on the Federal Reserve System."

Perhaps we are slowly learning that the stock market is indeed the "two-way affair" that Thomas describes. But this knowledge does little to diminish its influence or allure. The stock market is at once the circulatory system that lets money flow into business and industry, the maker of easy-money dreams, and the devastating force that can take it all away in one desperate hour. To play the stocks is to acknowledge all of this—consciously or not.

Chronology

1637	Prices for tulip bulbs bottom out after several years of rampant speculation in Holland
1792	The first incarnation of the New York Stock Exchange is born when 24 Manhattan brokers agree to trade exclusively with one another on May 17
1817	Now called the New York Stock and Exchange Board, the securities trading entity moves into its first permanent home at 40 Wall Street
1869	Speculation in gold triggers "Black Friday" on Wall Street on September 24
1907	Money panic at New York City banks threatens to shut down NYSE; J. P. Morgan and a group of bankers agree to pool emergency funds to keep banks from going under and keep Exchange open
1924–26	Speculation in Florida real estate drives prices to a peak before they start bottoming out
1924–29	A pooling syndicate that includes William "Billy" Durant successfully bulls up stock prices on the NYSE; prices for farm products drop 30 percent
1928	Herbert C. Hoover elected 31st president of the United States
1929	Dow-Jones Industrial Average reaches a high of 381 points and experiences its busiest day of trading to date on September 3; the Dow closes at a record 353 points on October 10; "Black Thursday," October 24, is marked by frantic selling, stemmed by organized support; the market's decline continues on "Black Tuesday," October 29, at which time some 16.5 million shares change hands
1930	Hawley-Smoot Tariff is passed, placing 50 percent duties on goods imported to America
1931–2	Nearly 1,000 banks fail nationwide
1931–9	Drought and excessive cultivation of farmland lead to the formation of the Dustbowl, especially in the plains states; the drought ultimately affects agriculture in over half the states in the nation

1932   Bonus Army marchers driven out of Washington, D.C., by U.S. Army on July 28

1933   Unemployment reaches nearly 25 percent; Franklin Delano Roosevelt sworn into presidency on March 4; FDR implements the Hundred Days from March 5 to June 16; Dow hits low of 41 points on July 8

1934   The SEC is formed to oversee the stock exchange's practices

1935   The Works Progress Administration (WPA) places unemployed workers in jobs; the Social Security Act is passed

1941   United States enters World War II on December 8; the increased demand for defense industry workers helps end the Great Depression

1954   New York Stock Exchange tries to attract investors with a promotional campaign called "Own Your Share of American Business"; the market starts on a bull run

1958   Boom in market gets a lift from America's quest to catch up with the U.S.S.R. after it launches *Sputnik*

1982   Market starts on a five-year bull run

1987   Dow reaches record 2,722.42 points on August 25; on October 19, "Black Monday," the Dow drops 508.32 points and 604 million shares are traded

1999   Dow-Jones Industrial Average closes over 10,000 points on March 29

Glossary of Stock Market Terms

Bears—People who purchase stock with the expectation that its price will drop.

Bonds—A paper document issued as proof of money owed to the holder.

Bulls—People who anticipate a continued rise in stock prices.

Closing—The value of a stock at the end of a business day of trading.

Common Stock—Shares of ownership in a company that do not pay dividends.

Corner—Ownership and control over a large enough portion of a given stock to influence its price.

Dividends—Money paid to investors when a company returns a portion of its profits.

Dow-Jones Industrial Average—A well-known index of the stock market's value that is derived from the average stock prices of 30 leading companies listed on the New York Stock Exchange.

Interest—a charge for borrowed money, usually a percentage of the amount borrowed.

Margin—Amount of cash presented as an advance fee for the purchase of a stock.

Point—A means of measurement for quoting stock prices.

Preferred Stock—Shares of ownership in a company, for which the owner receives dividends before common stock holders do.

Rediscount Rate—The interest rate on that the Federal Reserve Board charges on loans to member banks.

Securities—Proof of stock certificate ownership.

Shares—Units in which stocks are sold.

Speculators—People who agree to take accountability for a considerable risk with the hope of making a profit.

Stocks—Evidence of ownership in a corporation separated into share units and symbolized by exchangeable certificates.

Trusts—Large conglomerate businesses that make it impossible for smaller, non-member companies to compete with them.

Bibliography

Egan, Jack, and Daniel P. Wiener. "Time to Get out of the Market?" *U.S. News & World Report* (31 August 1987): pp. 56–58.

Galbraith, John Kenneth. *The Great Crash of 1929.* Revised edition. New York: Houghton Mifflin, 1997.

———. *A Short History of Financial Euphoria.* New York: Penguin Books USA, 1993.

Glassman, Bruce. *The Crash of '29 and the New Deal.* Morristown, N.J.: Silver Burdett, 1986.

Hoyt, Edwin P. *The Goulds.* New York: Weybright and Talley, 1969.

Lawson, Don. *FDR's New Deal.* New York: Thomas Y. Crowell, 1979.

Meltzer, Milton. *Brother, Can You Spare a Dime?* New York: Facts on File, 1991.

Millichap, Nancy. *The Stock Market Crash of 1929.* New York: New Discovery Books, 1994.

The New York Stock Exchange. "Historical Perspectives of the NYSE." Available at www.nyse.com

Oliver, Charles. "After an Eight-Year Bull Market, What Happens if Stocks Decline?" *Investor's Business Daily* (25 May 1999): A-4.

Ross, Stewart. *Causes and Consequences of the Great Depression.* Austin, Texas: Raintree Steck-Vaughn, 1998.

Terkel, Studs. *Hard Times: An Oral History of the Great Depression.* New York: Pantheon Books, 1970.

Thomas, Dana Lee. *The Plungers and the Peacocks.* New York: William Morrow, 1989.

Vanos, Mark N. "Wall Street's Credibility Gap." *Business Weekly* (23 November 1987): 92–94.

Wiener, Leonard. "A Lifeboat, Just in Case." *U.S. News & World Report* (31 August 1987): 61.

Index

Index

KRISTINE BRENNAN is a writer and editor in the Philadelphia area, where she lives with her husband and two children. She holds a B.A. in English with a concentration in professional writing from Elizabethtown College. This is her fourth book for Chelsea House.

JILL McCAFFREY has served for four years as national chairman of the Armed Forces Emergency Services of the American Red Cross. Ms. McCaffrey also serves on the board of directors for Knollwood—the Army Distaff Hall. The former Jill Ann Faulkner, a Massachusetts native, is the wife of Barry R. McCaffrey, a member of President Bill Clinton's cabinet and director of the White House Office of National Drug Control Policy. The McCaffreys are the parents of three grown children: Sean, a major in the U.S. Army; Tara, an intensive care nurse and captain in the National Guard; and Amy, a seventh grade teacher. The McCaffreys also have two grandchildren, Michael and Jack.

Picture Credits